D0754357

CAPON
ON
COOKING

BOOKS BY
ROBERT FARRAR CAPON

Bed and Board
An Offering of Uncles
The Supper of the Lamb
The Third Peacock
Hunting the Divine Fox
Exit 36
Food for Thought
Party Spirit
A Second Day
Between Noon and Three
The Youngest Day
Capon on Cooking

CAPON
ON
COOKING

Robert Farrar Capon

Houghton Mifflin Company Boston

1983

Portions of this book have previously appeared, in slightly different form, in the *New York Times, Newsday,* and *Newsday Magazine.*

Copyright © 1983 by Robert Farrar Capon

All rights reserved. No part of this work may be reproduced or transmitted in any form or by any means, electronic or mechanical, including photocopying and recording, or by any information storage or retrieval system, except as may be expressly permitted by the 1976 Copyright Act or in writing from the publisher. Requests for permission should be addressed in writing to Houghton Mifflin Company, 2 Park Street, Boston, Massachusetts 02108.

Library of Congress Cataloging in Publication Data

Capon, Robert Farrar.
Capon on cooking.

Includes index.
1. Cookery.   I. Title.
TX715.C2416   1983   641.5   83-91
ISBN 0-395-34393-3

Printed in the United States of America

Q 10 9 8 7 6 5 4 3 2 1

To Helene and Harold
without whom, not nearly so much.

Acknowledgments

I want to acknowledge my gratitude to all those who in any way contributed to the confection of this book: Harold C. Schonberg, Nancy Newhouse and Alex Ward at the *New York Times;* Rhoda Amon, Don Jacobsen and Ken Spencer at *Newsday Magazine;* Lou Schwartz, Phyllis Singer, Peggy Katalinich, Marie Bianco and Sylvia Carter at *Newsday;* and last but far from least, my wife Valerie, who typed the entire manuscript at least twice and helped in preparing the index.

Contents

PART II

Branching Out Through the Seasons

Introduction

Domestic cookery labors under a difficulty that plagues no other art. The Glorious Company of Graphic Artists is recruited only from the ranks of those who want to, and presumably can, draw. The Goodly Fellowship of Musicians contains no one not willingly devoted to a life of warbling, plucking or toodling. And the Holy Church of the Thespians is composed exclusively of born actors who freely choose showing off in public as the vehicle for displaying their personalities and looks. But the Noble Army of Household Cooks consists almost entirely of conscripts press-ganged into service by the necessities of everyday life.

If you are of a critical cast of mind, that element of constraint will no doubt explain why the world has more bad cooks than failed artists of all other sorts put together. But there is a more felicitous interpretation. It could also point to an advantage this book seeks to capitalize on: since no other art so effectively requires its devotees to practice every day, there may be more hope for cooks than for the followers of any other muse. These essays are simply one household chef's attempt to turn cooking's necessity into the mother of something better than drudgery and tuna-noodle casseroles.

What is needed for that happy issue out of affliction, however, is more than just another compendium of recipes. When an apple tree is in trouble, the wise gardener stops thinking about apples and dedicates himself to feeding, spraying and pruning. Accordingly, when cooks find themselves bored with the results of their labors, it is time not for new methods of producing the pies they have lost interest in making but for deep remedies indeed.

As I see them, the restoratives called for are two. On the one hand, the roots of cookery need to be refreshed: our almost chronic inattention to raw materials must be dispelled by a good turning over of the caked soil of culinary prejudice, and our acute impatience with process must be overcome by a good dose of basic technique. On the other hand, the branches of our cookery — the lush eclectic growths that are fast leafing out American cuisine — demand care as well: inauthenticities need lopping off; promising new shoots must be given light and air to flourish in. Since the roots take precedence though, consider those first.

I passed too quickly just now over the necessity of the cook's work. Its inevitabilities need distinguishing. The obligation to have food at all lies upon us for the starkest of reasons: if we do not eat, we die. But the strange compulsion that leads us to do so many things to food before we ingest it springs from a happier necessity: we cook in order to make life worth living. The taproot of cookery is not the desperation of the belly any more than it is the gastrointestinal tract's vulnerability to the imagined dangers of raw food; rather it is the mind's thirst for delight — its lifelong and obsessive quest to discover, in everything it takes a shine to, unnecessary goodnesses, superfluous beauties and gratuitous truths. And it is just that intellectual fascination with food and cooking — plus an equally mental delight in all the physical processes involved — that separates the cooks from the hash-slingers.

Even gourmet hash-slingers. We have gone on too long acquiescing in the folly that *good* cooking (you have seen, believe me, the first and last appearance of the word *gourmet* in this book) can be written into recipes, or that it can be the inevitable result of following them slavishly. The ability to put notes down on a page and the knack of reading them off correctly no more guarantee artistry in cooking than they do musicianship in music. What is needed in both is not the dog-effort to get from notation to performance without making a mistake, but the peculiarly human concern to find the lurking delights, the hidden *playabilities* — without which, nothing.

Let me put my cards face up and say right at the start where I think the love of culinary play comes from: we are the only animals that cook our food because we are the only animals that God made in his own image. If you object to such a profound begging of nearly every question under the sun, bear with me. I do not mean a word of it solemnly — only seriously. And the most serious thing I have to say about God — after fifty-some years of living in a world full of aardvarks and artichokes, garlic and girls' knees, mushrooms and men's noses, zebras and zucchini — is that whoever was responsible certainly spent a lot of eternity simply playing around. Creation looks like nothing so much as the original wild party. And therefore when I come to assign a meaning to the text "let us make man in our image, after our likeness," my preference is to conclude that what the majestically plural Party of the First Part had chiefly in mind was that we should be *parties* of the second part — that our best productions would always look more like play than work.

And so they do, in cooking especially. How many long Sunday afternoons did the daughter of the first cook devote to fooling with the notion of the pot? How much abuse did she suffer for wasting her time? How often was she mocked for interposing a barrier between heat and meat? But how lucky for us she just larked her unnecessary way along. To think of cook-

ery without all of its equally needless variations on her theme
is to think of something that is hardly cookery at all: nothing
poached, braised, steeped or steamed; nothing sautéed, fried,
pan-broiled or baked. Nothing, in short, but the fly-ridden,
smoke-belching barbecue that we, having lost our sense of genuine play, now actually classify as fun.

No, without the refreshment of the delight that is cookery's deepest root, a good half, if not more, of humanity's minimum daily requirement of intellectual play is going to elude
us. The first part of this book therefore works the soil around
that root: it deals with matters like improvisation and invention
in the kitchen, with subjects like the making of meat glaze and
the use of bare hands in cooking, with stoves, freezers and the
hierarchy of wooden boards, with salt, scallions and garnishes
— and with recipes that feed the mind as well as the body.
Most of the chapters are based on pieces that originally appeared in the *New York Times;* a few were first published in
either *Newsday* or the Sunday *Newsday Magazine.* All of them,
however, are seriously playful, not grimly earnest. Solemn high
cooking is not the name of my game on Sunday afternoons.

Nourishing the roots of cookery, though, is only half the task,
especially in the case of current American cuisine. For if our
cooking in the 1980s has one characteristic that fairly leaps to
the eye of the beholder, it is its spectacular branching out into
the cookery of other nations. This burst of exotic growths has
been going on since the fifties, and it has been no mere histori-
cal succession of passing fancies. French, Italian, Chinese and
Thai cooking (to name only a representative handful) may
have swept over us in about that order, but the remarkable
thing about them is that, like the branches of a tree, they are
all flourishing together at this very moment. We have developed an eclectic kitchen — and other nations have copied us:
Japan, no less, claims it has the best Italian food in the world.

In plain truth though, America probably has the most catholic cuisine the world has yet seen. It is not just that pasta and sauces have become occasional party fare, or that half our homes have woks; it is that these once foreign items have actually been incorporated into everyday American cooking. Accordingly, the premise of the second half of this book is that all of these sometime culinary enthusiasms put together — along with everything that was here before they struck — are now in fact the cuisine of America. Indeed, it may well be that the peculiar genius of our cooks has always been their aggressive habit of borrowing. New England fish chowders, for example, are probably of Portuguese inspiration. In any case, it is a habit by which they have given the cookery of other tongues and nations a permanent home.

There are hand-wringers, of course, who decry the loss of truly American cooking, but I am not among them. I consider our proliferation of cooking styles a sign of basically sound culinary growth. I trust our instincts, you see. We may watch TV till our eyes fall out, or eat fast food to distraction, but our national character is such that we still recognize the first as trash and the second as junk. It's just that we reserve to ourselves the inalienable right to enjoy them as we would any other tasteless joke. If the viewers-with-alarm would bother to look at what actually goes on in American kitchens, their fears would be considerably allayed.

Not that we don't have bad cooking. We have lots of it: diet cookery that actually boasts of its starchless, saltless, sugarless, practically-everything-elseless dishes; and vegetarian cookery that only gives vegetables a bad name. But those things are hardly cookery, let alone serious attempts at a cuisine. They are intellectual fads, imposing a handful of irrelevant philosophical prejudices on a grandly material business. There is no need to berate them: they are their own punishment and they have no place in this book.

What does have a place is some pruning and bracing of these newer branches of our cuisine. Inauthentic recipes need to be cut out of the repertory and truly typical ones provided instead. "Cooking Italian" or "cooking Chinese" is never going to amount to much in a kitchen where the only spaghetti sauce is made according to a formula for red library paste, or whose oriental bag of tricks contains nothing but a bottle of soy sauce. To revert to the artistic metaphor: a good Irish composer will be one who has heard a lot of authentic Irish music, not just "How Are Things in Glocca Morra?"; a good English writer will have read more than comic-strip versions of Shakespeare. If we are going to make the cookery of other nations truly a part of our own — and at our best, that is precisely what we are up to — then the recipes we cook from should be as close as possible to the real thing.

Part Two of the book, accordingly, provides just such help: it consists of brief essays on current branches of American cookery followed, in almost all cases, by a solid sampling of recipes to support the limb in question. There is a Chinese feast, a Spanish picnic, a Japanese barbecue, a Thai dinner, an Italian sauce-out. Most of these pieces first saw light in the Sunday *Newsday Magazine;* a smaller number, in the *New York Times.* They are arranged here according to the seasons, natural and liturgical, of the year — beginning, happily enough, with Christmas.

Take them, then — and in the fine phrase of the old prayer, "read, mark, learn and inwardly digest them." Indeed, if you are any kind of red-blooded American cook, you will undoubtedly want to whip up a batch of them as well. After all, they're *our* dishes now.

PART I

Refreshing the
Roots of Cookery

1

Improvisation

Humankind can be divided many ways — into male and female, children and adults, cat persons and dog lovers — and no doubt most of the distances we thus put between ourselves remain stubbornly unbridgeable. But the gulf fixed between cooks who can improvise and cooks who can't may not be as great as it seems. In fact, it may not be a chasm at all, but only a case of vincible ignorance. If bookbound cooks would learn to get their noses out of the printer's ink and into the air, they might be surprised at what they can produce.

For everyone, cook or not, is already rich in olfactory experience. You are walking along a street, for example, or emerging from an apartment house elevator and suddenly the odor of cooking bursts upon you. Reactions vary, of course. Tripe at the boil is only minimally enchanting; members of the cabbage family are not known for expiring gracefully. But given half a chance, the nose rises to the occasion: at certain times in delight at recognizing the familiar (scampi! curry! *coq au vin!*); at others in awe at the mystery of true greatness (My, my! What in the world could that be?).

With ordinary mortals, this piquing of the nose's curiosity leads to little. Unless they have time and money for the restaurant food thus sniffed, or the nerve to press strangers' doorbells and cadge dinner, they proceed to their appointed kinds of meal and evening as if nothing had occurred. But when the experience befalls a cook? Ah! That's what makes spontaneous music in the kitchen; for it separates the improvisers, who can turn a scent into a dish, from the recipe-followers, who can't cook a thing without notes.

Culinary genius, of course, goes far beyond both. André Previn's comment on Duke Ellington gives the measure of supreme talent in any art: "Stan Kenton can stand in front of a thousand fiddles and a thousand brasses and make a dramatic gesture and every studio arranger can nod his head and say, 'Oh, yes, that's done like this.' But Duke merely lifts his finger, three horns make a sound, and I don't know what it is."

Still, just as most of us wouldn't sneeze at the studio arranger's ability to reproduce certain stock musical patterns, so we shouldn't look down our noses at the comparable skill in cooking. Admittedly, it isn't the key to the culinary empyrean; but then it isn't mere book-cooking either. And the best thing about it is that, to a considerable degree, it can be acquired. All that's needed is a nose and a memory. With a little practice, any cook can learn to say of a surprisingly wide range of culinary effects: "Oh, yes, that's done like this."

True enough, it takes more than a sense of smell to make a cook: without good hands, a good eye and a good palate, no one ever goes all the way to the top of the ladder. But without a remembering nose, even the first rung will be a struggle. What we call taste is mostly smell. The mouth discerns only sweet, sour, salt and bitter; the nose picks up the rest. More than that, when we recollect a specific dish (at least a "made" dish — one that is a composite of several ingredients and not just a single item heated up), the aspect we most vividly recall is usually not the main ingredient but the aromas given off by the various seasonings. In calf's liver Veneziana, it's the Veneziana that the memory latches onto; without the Bourguignon, escargots could hardly be kept in mind.

When you cook, therefore, you will not go far wrong if you pay primary attention to the smells you produce — and of course, to the necessity of remembering how to produce them. That holds true whether you are following a recipe or faking out a dish as you go along; but because improvisation is the more open-ended process, let us use that, and not the production of a known dish, to illustrate the process.

Assume, for the purposes of this exercise, that your improvised dish will have but two principal ingredients: the uncooked chicken wings you happen to have on hand and the canned tomatoes with which you are disposed to sauce them. Not that the dish will contain nothing else. Far from it. You may use a dozen items or more before you are done, but — and this is the point of the exercise — every last one of them will be considered a *seasoning;* and of each, the nose alone will be the ultimate arbiter and judge.

Finally, since these olfactory judgments will normally be rendered in the order dictated by the cooking process, let us simply agree to a not unreasonable version of that order. The improvising nose will consider first which grease to use; second, what other meats, fish or vegetables to add; third, what additional liquids, if any, are called for; and fourth, what herbs and spices should be included. In practice, of course, the cook's mind tends as much to flit erratically among these categories as to proceed step by step through them; but in either case they will serve nicely. Nose at the ready, then: smell!

Grease. You eliminate the nearly odorless (soy oil) and the vaguely so (corn oil) and with your mind's nose you sniff the following for affinity with chicken and tomato: olive oil, peanut oil, butter, lard, bacon fat, chicken fat. In the process, you discover something not only about the various fats but about the dish that so far hardly exists in your mind. Chicken fat is eliminated as mere duplication of flavor, bacon as too much like the pasta *all' Amatriciana* you had two nights ago, lard as too Northern European and peanut oil as too Chinese. You are down to a choice between olive oil and butter, and you are moving rapidly in the hitherto unsuspected direction of something Continental but southern. One more mental sniff at the butter and that too goes by the board. You note in yourself a disposition to have a certain punch to your putative dish: it must be not just graceful, but well muscled too. Olive oil it is then. And either Spanish or Greek oil, at that: once again, you note an aversion this evening to understatement.

On then to the *meat, fish* and *vegetable* seasonings. You are hovering, obviously, around the Mediterranean: let us try to flush the dish lurking below your consciousness with a random sampling. Garlic? Naturally; but something more, too: you do not wish to stop at *marinara.* Onion? Probably. Mushrooms? You think not. Capers? No. Anchovy? Ah, that would propel you straight to *pizzaiola.* Anchovy, then? Alas, no, *pizzaiola* means oregano: you do not mean to make it *that* robust. Ham, perhaps? Probably not, for the same reason. You decide to let it go at that, and you catch a cerebral whiff of the dish so far produced: chicken wings browned nicely in good olive oil, then chopped onion and minced garlic stirred in till they too are a good color. Fine. The question now comes on the deglazing of the pan.

Liquids. Vinegar? Possibly; but perhaps that's over-punchy too. Wine? Why not? White or red? White. (That was, you note, not only a quick decision, but one that made you think, unaccountably, of rosemary. What *is* it that's in the back of your mind?) Stock? Certainly, if it's reduced enough. But white or brown? Not brown, you think; that would be back to *pizzaiola* again. Cream? No; you have a leaner sauce than that in prospect. Very well, then; you deglaze the pan with some French Colombard, reduce both it and a cup or so of chicken stock to next to nothing and finally stir in the tomatoes, crushed.

Accordingly, there comes at last the question of *herbs* and *spices.*

Rosemary? Yes; it must have occurred to you for good reason. Parsley? Obviously. Cinnamon — in the Italian manner, with a bit of lemon rind? Maybe; but you suspect that wasn't it. Paprika and allspice — or yet more cinnamon? No; the Middle East consists even less with your expectations. Fennel, tarragon? Negative again; that would be to stray in the irrelevant direction of lobster *à l'Américaine.* Sage? Ah, yes, that was *it!* And, by George, all the rest of the Turtle Herbs: basil, marjoram, rosemary, thyme and sage — rendered memorable by an acronym formed from the words Brooklyn-Manhattan Rapid Transit Subway (later shortened to BMT), and made unforgettable by countless platefuls of your oldest and best-loved recipe for tripe. Behold therefore the dish never before served on land or sea, but now fully realized by the unaided nose: *ailes de volaille à tortue* — or, more humbly, chicken with tripe sauce. Either way, though, a triumph of improvisation: something you always had in mind but never knew until a reminiscent sense of smell brought it forth.

For the record, here are some of the other "arrangements" your nose might have had in memory but rejected, bypassed or transcended in arriving where it did. They are listed alphabetically; all of them, one way or another, are tomato-based. Kept in mind, they enable the quick-scented cook to say with confidence, "Oh, yes; that's done like this."

A l'Américaine (lobster or shrimp) — Butter; onion, a little garlic; white wine, cognac, reduction of tomatoes; tarragon, bay leaf, parsley.
All' Amatriciana — Olive oil, plus fried bacon dice; garlic; tomato sauce; black pepper, red pepper.
Alla Puttanesca — Olive oil; garlic, anchovies, black olives, capers; tomato sauce, stock; parsley.
Armenian (lamb or beef) — Butter; onion, garlic; stock, reduc-

tion of tomatoes; paprika, allspice or cinnamon, black pepper, parsley.

Chinese (shellfish) — Peanut oil; ginger, garlic; saké or sherry, ketchup, soy sauce, stock; scallions, coriander leaves.

Creole (meat or shellfish) — Olive oil; garlic, onion, green pepper, chopped green olives; tomato sauce, brown stock; thyme, parsley.

Fra Diavolo (meat or seafood) — Olive oil; garlic, lemon rind; white wine, reduction of tomatoes; basil, rosemary, oregano, stick cinnamon, red pepper.

Greek (broiled fish) — Olive oil; sliced onion, sliced fresh tomatoes; white wine or ouzo; fennel, oregano, black pepper.

Marinara — Olive oil; garlic; reduction of tomatoes; parsley.

Milanese — Olive oil; garlic, anchovies; white wine, tomato sauce; dill.

Mushroom — Olive oil, butter; fried diced salt pork, mushrooms; tomato sauce, cream; parsley, black pepper.

Niçoise (seafood) — Olive oil; garlic, anchovies; white wine, reduction of tomatoes; capers, lemon slices, black pepper.

Pan Roast (shellfish) — Butter; chili sauce, Worcestershire sauce, lemon juice, cream; celery salt, paprika.

Pizzaiola (meat) — Olive oil; garlic, anchovies, parsley, black and green olives; white wine, brown stock, tomato sauce; oregano.

Provençale — Olive oil; garlic; reduction of tomatoes; black pepper.

Spanish — Olive oil; onion, garlic; reduction of tomatoes; parsley.

2

Bare Hands in the Kitchen

It is the ultimate kitchen gadget. It serves as a juicer for lemons, oranges and grapefruit, and as a combination seed remover and pulp crusher for tomatoes. It functions as a bowl scraper, an egg separator and a remover of unwelcome particles — the stray bit of eggshell, the odd grain of black rice — from mixing bowl or saucepan. It is a thermometer capable of gauging temperatures up to 500 degrees Fahrenheit and, in addition, is a measuring device for dry ingredients in amounts from 1 tablespoon down to ⅛ teaspoon or less, and for whatever liquids may be called for in the cooking of grains and stocks. It can be used as tongs for removing hot cup custards from the oven, as a mixer of water into pastry dough and as a kneader of bread. Best of all, it cleans up in a trice, presents no storage problems, will not chip, rust or tarnish and, if it cannot be said to be unlosable or indestructible, it nevertheless comes with a lifetime guarantee to remain the one household convenience you will have the least desire either to lose or to destroy.

It is, of course, the human hand.

But that is to proceed too quickly. For while it is a truism that good cooks have "good hands" (even to say the word evokes visions of Chinese chefs wielding cleavers at machine-gun speed, of old delicatessen proprietors slicing a side of nova into incredibly wide, paper-thin sheets, of great-aunts rolling *pâte brisée* into perfect circles with a French pie pin), those triumphs of technique are not what is being praised here. Not everyone — not even every serious culinary practitioner — is endowed with the eye-hand coordination needed to become the Itzhak Perlman of the cutting board or pastry table.

This essay, in short, is not about cooks who handle the tools of their craft brilliantly. It is about those who craftily use bare hands as their preferred tool.

The proclivity is recognizable early in life. Indeed, it is probably true that good cooks turn out invariably to have been children who played with their food. Beginning with the modeling of mud pies and proceeding through the palpating of mashed potatoes and the sculpting of print butter, they arrive quickly at a wisdom few adults retain. Before the age of five they know by experience that for any gastronomic purpose, from the liberation of the last dab of mustard in the jar to its distribution evenly along the hot dog, from the dissolution of cocoa in the cup to the removal of batter from the bowl, fingers were indeed made before forks — and fine hands, be they Italian, Chinese or French, before the food processor.

Consider therefore the culinary handinesses with which we began. You have, let us say, a batch of cup custards in the oven. They sit cheek by jowl in scalding water and they are done to a turn. How will you remove them expeditiously? With a potholder? No, for the only two things a potholder will infallibly get a grip on are the water in the pan and the custard in the cup next to the one you are grappling with. With tongs, then? Again no: the last time your tongs were seen was a year ago August during a corn boil. You remove them instead with your hands.

The technique is as follows. First, as close to the oven as possible, you prepare a space for setting them down. Then, holding all five fingertips against an ice cube or under cold water long enough to chill them, you shake the water off, grasp the first custard by the rim and remove it quickly to the counter. After that, you simply rechill your fingers before each subsequent cup. At no more than ordinary cruising speed, you will probably get them all out in twenty seconds or less — and feel hardly a twinge of heat in the process.

On the other hand, suppose you have a lemon to squeeze or a half-dozen superannuated grapefruit to juice before terminal rot sets in. What do you use for the lone lemon? The squeezer? Why? So it can sit in the sink for the rest of the afternoon and stare back at you? And what for the six grapefruit? The same squeezer? When it is already too small to deal even with an orange? No. Instead, you use . . . but watch.

Cutting the fruit in half crosswise, you pick up one half with the hand of your choice and you configure the less favored hand into a suitable extractor. For lemons, limes and very small oranges, this is done by holding the tips of three or five fingers tightly together and using them as the cone of the squeezer. For large oranges and small grapefruit, you form a larger cone by making a peculiar fist: the second joints of your index, middle and ring fingers are thrust upward into door-knocking position and the fruit thrust down upon them for squeezing. For the largest grapefruit, you make a true fist and use the base knuckle of your forefinger as the apex of the cone.

How do you get out the seeds? Why, with your hand's built-in particle removers, naturally. But if that much is obvious, other such uses of the digits deserve comment. For example, to remove a bit of shell from a bowl of egg white, two maneuvers are possible. The first is the single-finger pinion: you attack the offending particle from above with a forefinger and, having pressed it firmly against the bottom of the bowl, you drag it up and out along the side. Alternatively, and better, there is the two-finger flanking technique: the tips of the middle and ring fingers are held together side by side and the scrap of shell gently bracketed by them before being pounced on.

Needless to say, there will always be cavilers who claim to have considered these processes and found them disappointing. The hand, they will insist, is only a good, not a great, particle remover. But what they have not considered is that in most human pursuits (politics and parenting spring immediately to mind) what is in fact offered to us for choice are not great performances as opposed to good ones, but only moderate accomplishments as opposed to none at all. Let them try using spoons for a while. Why, a politician will sooner not pick up a contribution than a spoon will successfully pick up a . . .

But to continue. An egg broken into the cupped, slightly separated fingers of one hand easily sorts itself out into the white that runs through the fingers and the yolk that rests upon them. A tomato, if you cut it crosswise and probe its crevices with your fingertips, will yield up its seeds without a fight. And the same tomato, if held well down in the pot and squished energetically through the fingers of a strong fist, will enter into the stew coarsely crushed without once making a mess of the chopping board. In all of these, one pass of the hands under the water tap plus one wipe on the apron is the sum total of the cleanup necessary.

If, however, the instances so far given strike you as too rough and ready, consider the hand as measuring device. "Ah, but," you say. "How can mere flesh and bones be a substitute for neatly nested sets of metal spoons or for the full armamentarium of glass and plastic cups?" Well, to be honest, there are respects in which they can't. The hand has no skill to match the cunning with which the half-teaspoon hides, no fury to equal the smashing vengefulness of the glass measure dropped in scorn, no selflessness to compare with the plastic cup's enthusiasm for immolating itself on the dishwasher heating element. But in the most important respect, it is more than a match for them all: you can measure as accurately by hand as by anything. All it takes is practice.

To acquire the skill, you promise yourself to give your measuring spoons only one more week's houseroom. During the first four days of that week, you make a point of emptying every last measured spoonful of any ingredient into your hand before you add it to the dish. (In the case of 1 teaspoon or less, you place it in the middle of your palm; in the case of 1 tablespoon you place it in the "spoon" formed by your fingers when they and your thumb are held tightly together and cupped.) Then you look at it and say to yourself, "This is a tablespoon — or a teaspoon, or whatever." Soon enough you will know with surprising accuracy what each amount looks and feels like in your hand.

Accordingly, during the last three days of the week, you proceed to phase two of the course: you measure the ingredient into your hand and then check your accuracy by placing it in the spoon before proceeding further. After that — and with only a ten-second refresher course every six months or so — you are, as man was meant to be, the measure of all things.

Even, it should be added, the measure of quantities the hand is too small to hold. How do you know how much liquid to put into a potful of rice or bulgur wheat? You rest the tips of your fingers lightly on the leveled surface of the grain and add water or stock until it just reaches the first joint of your middle finger. End of subject. How much water do you add to bones to make stock in the first place? You press your hand, palm down, on top of the bones and fill the pot till the entire back of your hand is covered. Once again, you yourself are the sovereign gauge, not words in books or marks on gadgets.

Or even the supremely questionable numbers on oven dials and French-fryer controls. To learn to assess baking temperatures, you take a vow to thrust your hand into the preheated oven every time you are about to slide in a dish: you put it well in and hold it there for a brief but fixed period of time ("Thousand-and-one, thousand-and-two, thousand-and-three" will do nicely). If you pay attention for a week to the subsequent performance of your oven — and, of course, to the initial bearableness or unbearableness of the heat on your hand — you will soon come to a knowledge of exactly what a slow, medium, fast or very hot oven feels like. Or, finally, if you want to learn how hot the fat in the fryer is, you put the end of a wooden chopstick into the oil: after a few experiments, the speed with which the hot fat begins to drive fine steam bubbles out of the wood will tell you all you need to know about frying temperatures. I know. That last is not a use of the bare hand. But after all, even a marvel has limits.

From there on, though, the subject is literally in your hands. Just so you use them — picking up in them everything that won't bite or burn you first; touching, poking, feeling and hefting with them everything but what may do you a mischief if you handle it at all — you can hardly go wrong. The manual delights by which childhood let you in at the front door of humanity have come, in your ripeness and perfectness of age, around to the back of the house. Don't be afraid to let them in.

And, to help you do just that, here are three five-finger exercises in routine cookery. I honestly believe that once you make these items by hand as suggested, you'll never use any other method.

MAYONNAISE

1 egg
Salt
Dry mustard
Cider vinegar (or white wine vinegar)
Corn oil
Olive oil

Break the egg into an electric blender (not a food processor). Measure out ½ teaspoon each of salt and dry mustard, using the palm of your hand as suggested above, and add them to the egg.

Cupping your fingers together as suggested for measuring tablespoonfuls, hold them over the blender, and add 2 tablespoons of vinegar.

Run the blender at high speed and add corn oil in a thin, steady stream until the mixture becomes thick enough to begin rejecting the oil.

With the blender still running, add three generous splashes of olive oil one at a time, working each one into the mixture with a rubber spatula before adding the next. If the mayonnaise is still too thin for your taste, add additional splashes of olive oil in the same way until the desired consistency is reached. *Makes 1½ to 2 cups.*

Cleanup: one blender, one spatula. (Your hands are cleaned automatically in the washing.)

UNCOOKED TOMATO SAUCE FOR PASTA

6 fresh, ripe, large tomatoes
1 lemon
2 cloves garlic
Salt
Fresh basil leaves
1 pound vermicelli
Pepper
Olive oil

Boil 6 quarts of water. Turn off the heat, drop in the tomatoes, and let them stand for a few minutes. Fetch them out with a slotted spoon, run cold water over them, and peel off the skins. Start up the water again in time to cook the vermicelli.

Slice the tomatoes in half crosswise and, holding the halves cut side down in one hand, probe the crevices with the fingers of the other hand so that the seeds and juice run out. Drink the juice.

Break the tomato halves into a serving bowl by squeezing them out between the fingers of your fist.

Cut the lemon in half crosswise and, holding it over the bowl in your strong hand, squeeze out each half into the cupped fingers of your other hand. Let the juice drain through your fingers, leaving the pits behind.

Peel and mince the garlic cloves, and add them to the bowl, along with a generous ½ teaspoon salt (or to taste).

Tear up as many basil leaves as you like, and add.

Mix well, adjust seasonings to taste, and serve over hot, drained vermicelli that has been seasoned with freshly ground black pepper and a generous coating of good olive oil. Pass additional salt, pepper, olive oil and basil leaves at the table. *Serves 4.*

Cleanup: one pot, one knife, one colander, one serving bowl (and hands as before).

SWEDISH SHORTCRUST
(For fruit tarts)

Pastry or cake flour
Sugar
Baking powder
1 stick salted butter, plus the empty butter box
    (opened at one end)
1 egg

Fill the butter box ⅚ full of flour, top it up with sugar, and add 1 teaspoon baking powder, measured in the palm of your hand.

Empty the dry ingredients into a mixing bowl, and discard the free 2-cup measuring box.

Mix the dry ingredients thoroughly with your fingers, add

the stick of butter, and work it thoroughly into the mixture with your fingers.

When the butter is uniformly distributed, break the egg into the mixture, and work it in with your hand until you have a smooth paste. (This will be a bit untidy at first, but by the time the paste is properly mixed it will come away cleanly from both hands and bowl.)

Press the paste with your fingers into a suitable quiche pan, flan ring or pie plate, and fill it ad lib with sugared fresh fruit in season. Bake in a moderate oven until nicely browned.

Cleanup: one mixing bowl. (Hands? Just wipe them and enjoy the way they smell: they've had a free moisturizing treatment.)

3

The Secret of the Sauce

It is no exaggeration to say that cookery has just been through a reformation. *Nouvelle cuisine,* with its protests against old ways and its emphasis on freshness — with its insistence on unfloured sauces, its borrowings from the Orient, and its featuring of exotic ingredients — has left a permanent mark on the history of gastronomy.

And yet. As with so many reforms, it is the exotica of the movement, and not its solid accomplishments, that have captured the popular imagination. Turbans of flounder with blueberries and melon balls roll regularly off domestic assembly lines; the kiwi has become a cliché; green beans, uncut, untender, and unstrung, threaten to become the definition of dining; and walnut oil and raspberry vinegar are practically a bore.

But alas, the intense, satiny *nouvelle* sauces — those self-thickened quintessences of meat or fish that are the cuisine's crowning achievement — have yet to find their way into the home. It is a lamentable omission, and it is high time we did something about it. Herewith, therefore, an inside track to the reformation's most notable reform of all.

The secret of such unfloured sauces, in one word, is *reduction:* the boiling down of saltless but otherwise adequately flavored stock to one tenth or one twentieth of its original volume, so that, with most of its mere water carried off as steam, it becomes a concentrate of natural gelatines, acids, salts and aromatics.

The reason why so few such sauces grace the average board is not far to seek. The household cook (usually in a hurry) working at home on the familial range (frequently short on heat) is not about to stand around on one foot waiting for a quart or so of liquid to seethe its way down to three tablespoonfuls.

Fortunately, however, the solution to the problem is something neither recherché, nor expensive, nor even *nouvelle*. It is, in fact, one of the oldest, cheapest culinary short cuts in the world: Meat Glaze, or *glace de viande*. Admittedly, it takes time to make up a batch of this wonder worker; but once you have a bagful of meat-glaze cubes in your freezer, your days of weak and pasty sauces are over for good.

Let me tempt you with two visions. First, picture yourself at the stove. You have just finished sautéing . . . whatever: a pair of chicken breasts; two shell steaks; a brace of lamb chops; some scallopine of veal; a few flounder fillets; a fistful of shrimp. You remove them before they are quite done, deglaze the pan with a little minced onion and a splash of white wine, add heavy cream, boil it down a bit, check the salt, and finally return the main ingredient to the pan to heat through. Then, all anticipation, you taste the finished dish. It should, of course, be a triumph, a grand harmony of all its excellent parts. But it isn't. It is a ragtag group of flavors that have failed to organize themselves into a taste. It is a substance without an essence; a body without a soul. It is . . . well, let us say it plainly . . . just one more pan gravy.

On then to the second vision. It differs from the first in only two particulars. When you pour in the cream, you also add some cubes from your treasury of meat glaze. And when you taste . . . well, that I leave you to find out for yourself. Suffice it to say that your estimate of your own kitchen will go up by at least two stars.

How is this marvel made? Briefly, you boil down strained, defatted, unsalted stock (ten quarts, more or less) until it is a pint or so of brown, gelatinous syrup. Then you pour the syrup into an ice-cube tray (without the divider) and refrigerate it overnight. In the morning, you remove it from the tray by loosening one end and pulling the whole out in a single, marvelously elastic piece.

Before cutting it into cubes with a knife, however, stop. There are some things in this world that cry out to be relished before they are used. This . . . this *thing* you have just extracted from your ice-cube tray: it is like no other natural object on earth. To be as unpoetic as possible, it is not unlike the sole of a rubber beach sandal; but the comparison only underscores the differences. *Glace de viande* is heavier, yet more supple; it is a glorious natural brown, not a vile artificial one; it has a sheen like French polish; and as if all this were not enough, it is irresistibly good to eat.

What does it taste like? Well, to be honest, not like very much at first. But once the warmth of the mouth has begun to dissolve it . . . ah! It is the very soul of meat. Better yet, though not a grain of salt was used in its manufacture, it is perfectly seasoned with the native salts of its ingredients. But best of all, it enters into happy combination with almost any liquid in the saucier's book, providing an instant body that only long reduction could otherwise produce.

Consider: *glace de viande,* when properly made, is already at a reduction of some twentyfold. In other words, just three tablespoonfuls of it will bring almost a quart of plain hot water back up to the intensity of the broth you began with. Imagine then what those same three tablespoonfuls will do to the half-pint of heavy cream that fared so disappointingly in our first vision. It will make not just pan gravy, not just *jus.* It will, in fact, make none of those watery, floury disappointments you have spent a lifetime's patience on till now. Instead, finally and for good, it will make *sauce*.

The skeptic, of course, will narrow his mind's eye and ask, "If meat glaze is all that good, how come practically nobody makes it?" The answer is simple: as elsewhere in life, the longer the project, the fewer the volunteers. Meat glaze may not require much "hands on" time, nor even very much watching, but it does take two days to get it from start to finish, so only the truly possessed take it on.

In the hope, though, that what has been said may provoke the requisite preliminary seizure, a method of making meat glaze follows. Coupled with the recipes appended, it should be sufficient to guarantee a permanent addiction. I know. I haven't done without it for years.

MEAT GLAZE
(Glace de viande)

10 to 15 pounds meat scraps, bones and fat *(see note 1 below)*
2 large onions, sliced
2 large carrots, peeled and sliced
2 large ribs celery, cut up
6 sprigs parsley
⅛ teaspoon thyme
¼ teaspoon savory
2 bay leaves
12 whole peppercorns
Cold water

Note 1. Use any and all bones and scraps, fat or lean, cooked or raw, from beef, veal, chicken or pork. Beef should predominate, and knuckle bones yield lots of gelatine, but you can achieve decent meat glaze with 15 pounds of almost anything. Do not, however, use cured meats (too salty), lamb (too strong), smoked meats (too pronounced) or, as far as I'm concerned, even turkey, though duck and goose are all right.

It is possible, of course, to go out and buy 15 pounds of beef and veal bones and make superb meat glaze. But it is unnecessary. Simply keep a meat-glaze scrap bag in your freezer and add to it all relevant leavings until you have accumulated enough for a batch. (Assure the dog he will get them eventually, so he needn't moon around trying to make you feel guilty about squirreling them away.)

DAY I

Rinse the bones, scraps and fat, put them in a roasting pan, and roast them at 375° for an hour or so, turning them over occasionally to brown on all sides. Add the onions and carrots and roast ½ hour more — or until they, too, are brown (but not black).

Transfer the contents of the roasting pan to a large stockpot (about 20 quarts). Rinse the pan carefully several times, scraping to loosen the caramelized particles. Add the water from each rinsing to the stockpot. Then add all the remaining ingredients, and cover everything with cold water to a depth of 1 inch. *Do not add any salt.* Cover the stockpot, bring it to a boil slowly, reduce it to a simmer, and cook it for 4 hours. At the end, strain off the broth into a deep pot (about 12 quarts), using a chinois or an ordinary strainer lined with damp cheesecloth. Cool quickly, and refrigerate overnight. Discard the solids — or feed them to the pets.

DAY II

In the morning, remove the hardened cake of fat from the top of the broth, leaving no particles behind. Discard the fat — or save it for French frying.

Bring the broth to a boil and continue boiling it over high heat, uncovered, until it is reduced to about a pint of viscous, brown syrup. (Depending on your stove, the process will take from 1 to 2 hours. *See note 2.*)

Pour the syrup into a clean ice-cube tray (with the divider removed) and chill it in the refrigerator (not the freezer) for six hours or more.

Remove the meat glaze from the tray by prying up one end and pulling it out (it will come away cleanly). Cut it into three strips lengthwise and into cubes crosswise. Bag the cubes in plastic and store them in the freezer till needed.

Note 2. In boiling down broth, you will find that it goes through four stages. In the first, it simply bubbles at its own level like any other soup. In the second, however, it becomes viscous enough to make a "head" of fine froth that will rise precipitately and possibly overflow the pot. During this stage, therefore, keep an eye on it. The third stage is reached when the broth becomes more viscous still and makes rather larger bubbles that do not rise so high. And in the last stage, the "head" disappears, the bubbles become very viscous indeed, and the danger of boiling over is replaced by the danger of boiling dry. Needless to say, through all the stages the level of the liquid goes down, the salinity goes up, the color deepens and the flavor grows more rich.

By way of providing you with some guidelines for the incorporation of *glace de viande* into your routine cookery, here is one recipe in which it plays a sovereign part. Adapt it freely. This general approach will produce excellent results with almost any sautéed meat or fish. By way of variation, coarse mustard or an herb (tarragon, chervil, basil, rosemary or green peppercorns) can be added along with the cream, or a few peeled, seeded and chopped fresh tomatoes can be put in as the wine begins to disappear. In any case, the meat glaze remains the all-harmonizing touch.

SAUTÉED CHICKEN BREASTS

4 skinless, boneless chicken breast halves (from two chickens)
¼ cup flour
2 tablespoons clarified butter (*see note 3 below*)
2 tablespoons regular butter
1 small onion, minced fine
½ cup dry white wine
½ pint heavy cream
2 tablespoons meat glaze
White pepper and salt to taste

Dredge the chicken breasts lightly with flour and shake off the excess.

Melt the clarified butter over high heat in a frying pan and sauté the breasts quickly on both sides, until they are delicately browned. Remove to a serving dish. (At this point, the centers should still be raw.)

Add the ordinary butter and minced onion to the pan, stir vigorously (still over high heat) and, when the onion just begins to brown, add the wine.

Boil the wine away to almost nothing, add the cream and meat glaze, and continue boiling until the sauce is slightly thickened. Add white pepper and salt to taste, and return the breasts to the pan. Lower the heat and let them cook for a minute or so more, until the centers are just "set" past the point of rawness. Do not overcook. Serve over rice or pasta. *Serves 2 to 4.*

Note 3. Clarified butter contains no milk solids and therefore does not burn the way ordinary butter does. It can, in fact, be heated as hot as cooking oil. The ordinary butter, incidentally, is added during the deglazing (and therefore cooling) of the pan because it serves to enrich and, along with the cream and meat glaze, to bind the sauce. It is one of the oddities of creation that butter and cream — two fatty substances — will, if cooked together, produce a satiny sauce with not a trace of free fat.

To make clarified butter. Put 1 pound of butter in a 1-quart measuring cup and stand the cup in a large, deep pot containing an inch of water. Cover and boil for 15 minutes. Remove the cup and allow the melted butter to separate quietly for 5 minutes. Remove any solids floating on top of the butter with a spoon (do not disturb the solids that have sunk to the bottom). Then carefully pour off the clear yellow liquid into a suitable container, and refrigerate. All the residues, by the way, can be put into another container and refrigerated as well. They still contain some butterfat — along with a great deal of salt — and are perfectly acceptable for seasoning vegetables. You just add little or no extra salt when you use them.

4

Invention

You have seen them. You may even have been one of them: cooks, standing motionless before the meat case or paralyzed in front of the produce display, all their menu-planning circuits shorted out, the only activity in their minds a prayer that Someone would invent a new animal, vegetable or fruit. As they see it, they have exhausted the possibilities of the ox, the sheep and the pig; worse yet, they feel exhausted by four months of asparagus cookery and a fresh-fruit season that has been stalled at strawberries since March.

Their problem, however, is due neither to a failure of invention on the part of the Creator nor to the unnaturally extended seasons now afforded by vegetables from California and fruits from Mexico. It is not that they have been denied a change of comestibles. They themselves have run out of recipes.

Consider. A lengthened produce season could as well be a blessing as a bore: any cook with 122 unique and different ways of preparing asparagus could confidently defy the entire alliance of March, April, May and June. And since recipes come from cooks before they come from books, anyone willing to spend spring inventing no more than a single strawberry dish per week would make the world eighteen concoctions the richer by the Fourth of July.

What is needed, therefore, is an inquiry into the process of culinary invention. Are the steps by which the concocting mind works shrouded in the mystery of genius and thus incommunicable? Or are they knowable and simply waiting to be reduced to didactic order? And if they are thus reducible, how in fact shall that order be expressed?

Take the question of genius first. No doubt certain culinary inventions were all but created out of nothing by sheer brilliance. But they are probably not the ones that come first to mind. Louis Diat invented vichysoisse; but far from being a creation *ex nihilo*, it was only a logical, if felicitous step up from potato soup. No, the true dishes *de novo* are almost certainly the work of unknown geniuses: the baked potato, by the first child to wait long enough to retrieve a tuber that had fallen in the fire; the strawberry shortcake, by the farmer and his wife who spent a springtime's worth of Saturday afternoons deciding how best to eat their way to oblivion.

The culinary discoveries of sheer genius, therefore, have most likely all been made "once or twice, or several times, by men whom one cannot hope to emulate." All is not lost, though: there is still necessity to mother invention. And the specific form of it most likely to call forth new dishes from ordinary mortals is the need for variety forced upon them by seasonal glut. It is precisely when asparagus has been served in all known ways that the time of the unknown is at hand. It is in the effort to head off the tenth strawberry tart in succession that the kitchen finally succeeds in producing something new.

Before going on to inventions based on those two gluts, though, take an example from a third, briefer instance of oversupply. In April, sport fishermen vie with each other to see who can unload the most gunny sacks full of mackerel on their neighbors' doorsteps. And if you are not only one of those neighbors but also a true cook, you will long since have acquired recipes to reckon with such largesse: poached mackerel in dill, wine, or shrimp sauce; baked mackerel in Breslin sauce;

sautéed mackerel roe with bacon; cold pickled mackerel; mackerel salad . . .

But suppose that in a given year all those grew dull before the mackerel showed any sign of giving up? Suppose that like . . . Demetrios, let us call him . . . the springtime presence of roe and milt in female and male mackerel respectively led you to look to those admitted oddities for possible culinary inventions. What did Demetrios do that you might learn from? Why, he cast his mind back over his cooking experience and came up with ideas for two new dishes.

For the first (obviously a relative of shad roe with bacon) he decided to take mackerel roe, wrap it in a thin slice of bacon, sprinkle it with lemon juice, then encase it in buttered phyllo pastry, chill it, and bake it in a hot oven. For the other dish (not quite so obviously a spinoff of brains in black butter) he would take the milt sacs, poach them in lemoned water for just the few seconds needed to "set" them, then sauté them quickly in browned butter, and deglaze the pan with capers and vinegar.

But enough. Time to convert an admittedly fishy example into an object lesson on invention with asparagus and strawberries.

The first thing the mind of any Demetrios will do is draw upon experience. All previous concoctions of asparagus will be reviewed, no prior presentation of strawberries left unexamined. With help from the clientele of your cuisine, you will determine not simply what recipes everyone is most fed up with, but also what aspects of old recipes seem still salvageable. Indeed, by that one step you will be halfway home: asparagus with hollandaise will have been given the gong as a cliché; but strawberries and brown sugar will remain a possibility, provided the new dish involves something more than simply dipping the one in the other.

Next, however, you take note of some of the distinctions your mind is employing as it works. You seem, for example, to have borrowed the thick/clear classification from soup cookery:

the asparagus with hollandaise was a *thick* presentation; the dipped strawberries, a *clear* one. (By contrast, asparagus with drawn butter would be clear, strawberries drowned in whipped cream, thick.)

Further, you have just tripped over another distinction: the principal ingredient of a dish is sometimes concealed, sometimes exposed. You inquire, accordingly, whether your strawberries will be *latent*, i.e., enclosed in something else, like Demetrios' roe in phyllo pastry; or whether your asparagus will be *patent*, i.e., like the milt, standing forth in proper form for all to see.

Finally, it occurs to you to ask whether the asparagus or the strawberries will come to the table *alone* or *with others*. This question, borrowed obviously from the confessional, derives from the fact that many of life's experiences become more considerable as they involve partners. A strawberry tart, solo, is only a strawberry tart; a strawberry and rhubarb pie with vanilla ice cream is a whole 'nother species of sin.

Putting all these distinctions to work, therefore, your mind moves to invention. After so many *patent* presentations of asparagus *alone* in *thick* sauces, you determine that your new dish will, first, be *clear;* second, contain *another* principal ingredient; and third, hold both items *latently* until knife and fork reveal them.

Settling the question of the other ingredient first (from Chinese cookery you remember the affinity of asparagus for garlic; from French, the classic chicken with forty cloves of garlic), you decide that garlic it will be — one clove for each spear of asparagus: the garlic first parboiled in a little salted water and butter, then the asparagus steamed briefly in the same pot. After that, the dish practically makes itself: three leaves of phyllo dough, buttered; five spears of asparagus and five cloves of garlic laid on top and brushed with lemon juice; the dough rolled up, buttered and chilled; and the pastries baked in a hot oven as quickly as possible.

As for your strawberry dish, you decide that it too will be *latent* and *with others* — but, for variety's sake, *thick*. You toy momentarily with several possibilities. Strawberry cheesecake you have done; but strawberries and ricotta with sugar and grated orange rind, wrapped in thin omelets? And warmed in a chafing dish with butter and Grand Marnier? Alas, no. That is a long way to go simply to reinvent the blintz. Better a shorter cut, you think: the old Denver Chocolate Pudding gambit from Fannie Farmer: a layer of anything put in the bottom of a baking dish, some biscuit mix spread over that, and the whole covered with an appropriate liquid. When it's baked, the liquid runs under the dough, giving you sauce, filling and biscuit all in one pan.

And so you come at last to your second invention: a pint of strawberries, hulled, sliced, sugared, and allowed to stand; a 9-by-9-inch baking dish, buttered; the berries drained of their juice, and spread in the bottom; dollops of ricotta, mixed with grated orange rind and sugar, and dotted about; a layer of biscuit dough put in place; brown sugar sprinkled on that; and a pint of heavy cream mixed with the strawberry juice, and poured over all.

What next, though, now that your inquiries have brought you to this point? Why, there is nothing for it but to make up both dishes, taking notes as you go and correcting in the crucible of practice any misperceptions you made in the armchair of theory. By way of a final example, therefore — a gift, as it were, from one Demetrios to another — here are the recipes with the corrections duly noted.

ASPARAGUS AND GARLIC IN PHYLLO PASTRY

24 garlic cloves, peeled
½ cup water
2 tablespoons butter

Salt to taste
Lemon juice to taste
24 spears asparagus (not too thin), upper parts only
12 sheets phyllo dough
¾ cup melted butter (or as necessary)
½ cup crumbled feta cheese

Put the first five ingredients in a deep saucepan and simmer, covered, for 5 minutes.

Tie the asparagus spears in a bundle and stand them, tips up, in the same saucepan. Return to the boil, cover, and simmer for 3 to 5 minutes (they should be undercooked at this point). Uncover and cool.

Layer up three sheets of phyllo dough, brushing each with melted butter; place six asparagus spears (three pointing each way) and six garlic cloves (*note 1*) at one end; add 2 tablespoons crumbled feta cheese (*note 3*), and sprinkle with some of the cooking liquid (*note 2*). Fold the end of the dough over the ingredients, forming them into a bundle, fold the sides of the dough over to enclose everything, and roll up neatly. Brush with melted butter. Chill, seam side down, for several hours.

Repeat the process with remaining ingredients, making four pastries in all.

Bake at 425° for 15 to 20 minutes, or until a good color.

Serves 4 generously as a luncheon dish (with, perhaps, some creamy scrambled eggs). *Serves 8* (if each pastry is cut in half crosswise) as a "vegetable" at dinner.

Note 1. The number of spears was changed to six per pastry when it became obvious that half a pastry would do as a dinner portion.

Note 2. It turned out to be simpler to get the butter and lemon juice into the finished pastries by including them in the cooking water and simply sprinkling *that* on the ingredients.

Note 3. The addition of feta occurred to Demetrios after he had made two of the four pastries. The two containing the cheese were pronounced definitely superior.

STRAWBERRY CHEESE PUDDING

1 pint strawberries, washed, hulled and halved
⅔ cup white sugar
Grated rind of 1 orange
Pinch of salt (or to taste)
1 cup ricotta cheese
1½ cups prepared biscuit mix
½ cup milk (plus a little more, to make a soft dough)
⅔ cup brown sugar
1½ cups heavy cream

Combine (*note 1*) the first five ingredients, and spread the mixture in the bottom of a buttered 9-by-9-inch baking dish.

Combine the biscuit mix with the milk, and drop the dough by spoonfuls on top of the strawberry-cheese mixture. Spread it out evenly with fingertips dipped in milk.

Sprinkle the brown sugar (*note 2*) over the dough, and pour the cream (*note 2*) gently, into a spoon, over all.

Bake at 350° for 45 to 50 minutes.

Serves 8 (*note 3*).

Note 1. Allowing the strawberries a preliminary maceration with sugar took too much liquid out of them. They tended to disappear in the finished dish.

Note 2. Likewise, incorporating strawberry juice with the cream turned out to be a poor idea. It mixed with the brown sugar and produced a final "sauce" that was not a good pink but rather an alarming mauve. Replacing the brown sugar with white, of course, would have solved the problem; but a) Demetrios didn't want to, and b) the top of the dish would have been less attractive.

Note 3. The pudding would probably serve sixteen delicate

eaters. It is not only *thick* but *weighty*. Nevertheless, for ribs that still have spaces for sticking things, it's a fine dessert.

For the record, incidentally, here is a deluxe version of the original inspiration for the asparagus pastries.

SHAD ROE IN PHYLLO PASTRY

2 pairs fresh shad roe
4 very thin slices bacon
Lemon juice to taste
Salt and pepper to taste
16 sheets phyllo dough
¾ cup melted butter (or as needed)

Separate each pair of roe carefully into two pieces, removing connecting tissue without piercing the roe sacs themselves. Salt each piece lightly, wrap it in a slice of bacon, and sprinkle it with lemon juice and pepper.

Layer up four sheets of phyllo dough on a board, brushing each sheet with melted butter. Place one piece of roe near the narrow end of the dough, and fold the end flap over it. Then fold the long sides of the dough toward the center to enclose the roe, brush the flaps with butter, and finish rolling up the dough.

Repeat with the remaining three pieces of roe, wrapping each in four sheets of phyllo dough.

Refrigerate the rolls thoroughly (or give them a short time in the freezer). The purpose of this step is to ensure that the center of the roe will still be slightly rare when the pastry is fully cooked. Overcooked shad roe, if it is not yet a federal crime, nevertheless remains a cardinal sin. This is one of the few dishes that helps you avoid it.

Bake at 450° until the pastry is nicely browned. *Serves 4.*

5

Stoves

This is the story of one man's quest for a good he loved but lost. True, the good was nothing more than an utterly responsive, passionately hot kitchen cooking surface. But his pilgrimage nevertheless followed the course of every genuine romance: boy meets stove, boy loses stove, boy gets stove. Or, to send the subject as far upstairs as possible, his was a drama of Original Righteousness, Fall, and Redemption: he began with innocence in the Eden of a six-burner, two-oven commercial gas range; he proceeded through a world of stove tops diabolically designed to prevent cooking; and he ended in a culinary paradise once again.

But I proceed too quickly. Our hero once was Adam: he took his rise as a cook in the Garden itself, with a Garland. His first feeble efforts — the odd egg, the occasional cutlet, the sometime singed green pepper — were made in the happy assurance that only his own skills needed perfecting. All else was well.

Oh, I know. Conditioned as you have been by the doctrine of evolutionary progress, you take a dim view of stories that begin with a golden age. "Surely," your nineteenth-century prejudice wants to say to me, "he only *thought* that stove was paradise. Men may indeed go through hardship to the stars, but they do not start at the stars. After all, how much did he really know about cooking then? Five sticks, three pieces of newspaper and a match would probably have met all the need for heat he ever had."

I am sorry, but I cannot subscribe to that. Only the concept of a Fall does justice to his facts. He came down from something great, not up from nothing much. Though my Adam may once have been an innocent at cooking, at least in that innocence he knew he *cooked*. He did not struggle through scrambled eggs over a gas burner that left the center of the pan cold. Soups boiled over, yes, and omelets burned; but by George they boiled fast, and by Heaven they burned evenly.

He did not misremember the Garden, then. True, most of his advances as a cook — like most of the achievements of humanity — occurred after he was cast out of it. But that only made him remember it the more. It was as if (to change the illustration) he had happily played chopsticks on the piano as a child and was then subjected to teachers who required him to play Chopin with mittens on. It can be done — badly, of course. And a certain amount of Chopin can probably be gotten under the belt in the process. But one does not, for all that, either forget the Garden or begin to think kindly of gloves.

So, to return to my narrative, he went forth to cook in the sweat of his face. Many stoves he met. Some came found in rented quarters, some he bought. But since on the one hand there never entered into the furnishing of any of his kitchens a single architect, developer, builder or landlord who had the least conception of what a cook does at a stove — and since on the other hand the Prince of Darkness had so arranged the stove business that the one thing he could never do with a prospective purchase was try it out — all the stoves of his exile were worth neither the finding nor the buying.

He suffered. More in mind, perhaps, than in fact; but who,

since Freud, will cast the first stone at him for that? There was longing: oh, for the golden days when a twenty-quart pot of water would boil in less than a week! There was frustration: why did he have woks, if not to brown meat quickly; why a stove, if not to heat woks hot? But why then did he have to put up with contrivances that turned out only five more Btu's than a fading romance? Why have to suffer gray beef drowning in its own juice?

Finally, though, there was outrage. Electric surface units might exasperate by their slowness and gas burners might infuriate by their spottiness, but for producing the highest dudgeon, nothing matched the ceramic stove top. Oh, the mindlessness of obtruding an *insulator* between heat and pot! Oh, the uselessness of a stove that heated only vessels with special, machine-flat bottoms! Oh, the fraudulence of a device, touted for cleanliness, that burned every smallest spilled drop! For the six months he put up with the monstrosity, he never knew whether his culinary disasters were inside the pot or out. In the end, it was either the stove or his sanity; at the very edge of breakdown, he frightened his landlord into taking it out.

Alas, however, the happy ending still was not to be. The gas surface unit that replaced it was yet another disaster: silly little ring burners with no center flames and hardly enough heat among the lot of them to melt an ice cube. He sulked. He schemed. He contemplated robbing a bank branch and buying his own stove. He priced commercial ranges and went back to sulking: he didn't know the location of enough branches to meet the tab. Besides, there wasn't room in his kitchen. He went back to scheming.

There was, of course, the possibility of a deluxe surface unit: they existed, they had good cast-iron burners, and they threw a fair amount of heat evenly. But that too went whistling: $450 was still too steep for him, straight or crooked. And so it

went, from pricey bad to extravagant worse, until one fine day
he found himself in, of all places, a candy kitchen.

And there, standing in a corner throwing enough heat to
melt pig iron, was the stove of his dreams. To call it unprepos-
sessing would be an understatement. It looked like a cast-iron
snare drum with three legs. It had a perforated top consisting
of removable concentric iron rings and it stood two feet high.
It was the burners inside, though, that finally stole his heart:
three separately controllable concentric rings, each with a double row of jets, producing a spectacular 60,500 Btu. Mustering
his courage, he asked the price: $320 list, the candy man said.
Our hero fainted on the spot.

Reviving, he went straight out and bought one. Its proper
name, he learned, was indeed a candy stove — though not only
confectioners used it. Delicatessens, bakeries and restaurants
often kept one around as an auxiliary for heating huge pots. In
any case, with very little adaptation, it served him well ever
after.

The adaptation consisted of only two things. The first was
the construction of a square wooden platform to bring the
stove's top to a height of 35 inches. The second was the fashion-
ing of three iron spacers to enable him to use the stove with a
20-inch wok. Details of both of these follow below, as do further comments on the stove's usefulness.

Let it suffice in conclusion, then, simply to count the bless-
ings his candy stove brought him. He has finally all the power
and responsiveness he needs for true cooking: the stove heats a
14-inch heavy aluminum skillet as easily as if it were an omelet
pan; it boils water for pasta in short order; it reduces twenty
quarts of tomatoes to ten in a trice; with a 20-inch wok in place,
it very nearly equals the efficiency of a commercial Chinese
setup; and, oriental cooking to one side, a wok in the candy
stove is the single most used piece of equipment in his kitchen:
it is a deep-fryer par excellence; it browns roasts and stew meat

with speed and without sticking or loss of juice; it will make chicken cacciatore for a reunion and boeuf bourguignon for a regiment . . .

But I make an end. Marvels described at a distance are only unbelievable. If you are any kind of cook, you will have to see this one for yourself.

DETAILS — CANDY AND BAKER STOVE
(Model CM-64)

MANUFACTURER

Unity Stove Company, Incorporated
232 East 125th Street
New York, New York 10035
Telephone (212)427-4848

SPECIFICATIONS

Removable top rings
20-inch-diameter top
23¼-inch height
20¼-by-26½-inch floor space
100 pounds shipping weight
Three-ring burner, individually controlled
Universal gas jets (natural gas or liquefied propane),
    adjustable after installation
All cast-iron stove
Price: $320.00 list (commonly discounted)

RATINGS

Natural gas: 60,500 Btu
Liquefied propane gas: 52,500 Btu

AVAILABILITY

The stove is sold by dealers in restaurant supplies. In New York City, many of these are located on the Bowery in the blocks between Houston and Delancey streets. The manufacturer does not sell at retail.

Before contemplating the purchase of this stove, check the applicable local building, fire, and other codes.

Proper venting and shutoff equipment may be required. In addition, it should be noted that, since the stove lacks a pilot light and since its valve knobs are exposed, it may be undesirable for use where small children will have access to it. Finally, it is an auxiliary to, not a substitute for, a standard four-burner stove top and oven (in effect, it is a single-burner stove and can handle only one pot, albeit a large one, at a time).

That to one side, it is a treasure. The top rings are so constructed (with perforations and baffles) that heating is uniform. With all the rings in place, the stove functions as an ordinary cooking surface. With the three center rings removed, the top becomes a well that will hold a wok 14 to 17 inches in diameter. To use a 20-inch wok, all the center rings can be removed. In this case, however, since the outermost rim has no perforations, it is necessary to contrive spacers to allow the heat to flow freely around the wok. Perhaps the simplest arrangement is to make three U-shaped hangers out of ½-inch strap iron and hang them over the rim before seating the wok. Alternatively, the hangers can be made from 2½-by-⅝-inch corner irons, bolted together thus:

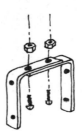

A serviceable platform for the stove can be made from 1-by-12-inch lumber, thus:

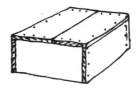

The top of the platform should be covered with sheet aluminum or some other fireproof material. If the stove is to be installed next to a wall or counter, the surfaces adjacent to it should be covered likewise with protective flashing.

The stove comes unfinished. A coat of stove polish applied from time to time will keep it both presentable and rust free.

6

Putting Wood to Use

One of the paradoxes in the American household kitchen is the way we make use of wood. On the one hand, there's plenty of it around: handsomely grained cupboards are commonplace; butcher blocks, pastry tables and whole islands of wood pop up everywhere; even dishwashers can be had with cutting boards on top of them.

Yet when it comes to putting wood to work in the everyday processes of cooking, we find it curiously underemployed. For one thing, those built-in wooden cutting surfaces are often treated more as décor than as part of the operation. The householder's principal consideration is how to keep them looking as if they never saw a knife, let alone a fiery pot. If you doubt this, simply volunteer your services someday in a friend's kitchen and put a hack mark or a frying-pan scorch on one of those tops. See how long the friendship lasts.

Alas, though, that's not all that's wrong. Wooden surfaces of the permanently installed type are usually just as permanently buried under pots, pans and crockery. But to make matters worse, they trick you into thinking you can use them for every task that calls for wood — a mistake that becomes painfully evident when today's strawberry tart pastry ends up tasting alarmingly of yesterday's garlic juice.

Accordingly, a well-run kitchen needs three separate and distinct wooden surfaces: one for onions and garlic, and for the host of vegetables and meats that can hold their own against such smells; another for dealing with fish and similar less smelly but still pronounced substances; and a third for pastry, bread, and whatever must not be contaminated by any odors at all. The solution? Old-fashioned, loose cutting boards.

Even if you have a whole kitchenful of built-in wooden counters, you need at least two such movable boards: the best and newest one for pastry only and the other for fish. That leaves you your counter top for onions and the heavy-duty abuse it's in the best position to take. Lacking installed wooden surfaces, of course, you need three boards — a number you achieve simply by demoting your first two and buying a brand-new pastry board.

In any case, when it comes to the rough jobs at the low end of this kitchen totem pole, the best of all possible wooden surfaces is one that, while it takes a bit of patience to come by, is more than worth the wait. It is the Chinese chopping block.

You acquire this paragon by keeping an eye and ear open for anyone who is felling a large maple tree, preferably 17 to 20 inches in diameter. You approach such a person with a suitable bribe and you ask him to cut you a 7-inch-thick section from the widest part. Then (perhaps with the help of a friend's belt sander) you make the top side perfectly smooth and install four rubber feet on the bottom. Behold, the world's finest hard-duty cutting surface — equaled in solidity and noise-absorbing qualities only by the professional butcher block, but not nearly the drain on the pocketbook.

Why is it so good? Well, to start with, its surface is end-grain wood, not face- or edge-grain. The knife bites *between* the fibers, not across them, thus doing both the block and itself a minimum of damage. Beyond that, it's movable without being flighty; and it can be stored — by the simple device of standing it on edge and pushing it flat against the backsplash — right out in the open. No other cutting surface can be at once so out of the way, so readily available, and so absolutely impossible to stand anything on.

The next time you hear the sound of a chain saw in the neighborhood, therefore, get your oriental cunning ready. The perfect chopping block is only a bribe away.

7

Freezing

In a time when so-called kitchen conveniences regularly go straight from overuse to underemployment without passing through sane utilization, the home freezer stands as a prime example of the sensible, time-tested appliance. Be it a 19-cubic-foot monster or only the top half of a two-door unit, it enables the cook, year round, to save practically anything and, in high summer, to make frugal use of nature's prodigality with vegetables. Whether they come from green-markets or from back gardens, from farm stands or from friends, it's the freezer that gives the harvest a home.

Alas, though, some of the literature on this simple, thrifty device seems bent on making its use both complicated and expensive. Special containers are apparently *de rigueur*. Hours, sometimes whole days, seem called for. The general impression given is that only a steadfastly High Church approach to freezing is respectable: unless one can match the Green Giant's mastery of the ceremonies, one is presumably a heretic, if not a heathen.

Herewith, therefore — on behalf of the vast majority of cooks, who have neither taste nor time for such fripperies — a resolutely Low Church method of freezing. It requires no equipment beyond a food mill, an ice pick and the pots, pans, graters and plastic bags you already have in the house; it takes the absolute minimum of time; and, as an unexpected gift, its products fit into freezer spaces as well as any. Its name? The Tombstone Method of Vegetable Preservation.

Its essence is twofold. It calls for the freezing of all vegetable items in either a completely or a partially cooked state (thus reducing the volume as well as concentrating the goodness of the substances to be stored). And it calls for the freezing of them in large, single slabs that, when solid, are broken up into baggable pieces with an ice pick. To see the method in practice, take the case of The Tomatoes of August.

Assume, if you will, that on some late-summer Saturday there sits in your kitchen a bushel basket of tomatoes. And pass, as irrelevant, the question of how they got there. Whether they were bought by you voluntarily, dumped on you unceremoniously, or simply provided to you by tomato plants that didn't know the meaning of quit, the fact is that they are there — and more than likely to proceed right on over the hill unless you do something about them.

And so you do. You select the largest pot (or pots) you own. You wash the tomatoes and, cutting out the stem ends and rotten spots, you put them into the pot, squishing each one with your hand as you go. When all are in, you crank up the heat under the pot, bring it to a boil and, stirring the contents now and then as you pass by, you boil the tomatoes down, uncovered, to about half their original volume. This takes a bit of time but little minding, so you catch up on your knitting, cat-napping or novel-reading.

When the tomatoes have been sufficiently boiled down, you put the entire contents of the pot through an old-fashioned, hand-held food mill (for example, a Foley Food Mill), catching the resultant purée in something suitable and discarding the skins and seeds. Then you simply pour the purée into a large, deep, metal (not glass) baking pan; you select a level space in your freezer (constructing one if necessary with ice-cream boxes and wedges of frozen pot roast); and you set the pan, uncovered, to freeze.

The next day, all you do is remove the pan to the sink, run a little hot water over the bottom, pop out the tomato-flavored headstone your efforts have produced and, placing it on a chopping board, you ice-pick it into squares or oblongs ad lib. Then you bag them (several to a bag), tie them with a twist, and return them to the freezer for storage. Behold! Three months' worth of robust tomato base-of-all-work.

Next, two variations. First, zucchini. This method has the distinction of being the only sensible way on earth of dealing with the great, green, Naugahyde-covered dirigibles that people invariably unload on your doorstep (or that you suddenly discover in a zucchini patch you thought you were keeping an eye on). You strip off the impenetrable skin with a vegetable parer. You split the monster in half and scrape out its seeds with a tablespoon. You grate its remaining flesh on the coarsest shredder you have in the house. You stir-fry the shredded zucchini in lots of butter (but not for too long — only till it's half-cooked). You pour the mixture into a metal baking pan, cool it, freeze it, de-pan it, reduce it to blocks with an ice pick, and bag and store it as you did the tomato purée. *Voilà!* A foundation for zucchini quiches, frittatas and sauces that takes up practically no room at all.

Second variation. Greens (spinach, escarole, Swiss chard, kale, collards, mustard, beet greens, whatever). Bring a few quarts of water to a boil in the largest pot you have. Wash the greens. When the water boils, put them in, pushing them down till they're all under water. When the water reboils, remove the pot to a (clean) sink, and run cold water into it till the greens are completely cooled. Drain; squeeze; chop them up as you like; put them into the now familiar metal baking pan; and freeze, de-pan, and so on, as before. *Ecco!* Greens to be glorified by garlic for a year.

One last word: label everything. One of the delusions of intelligent people is that once they have done something the favor of knowing it, they think it thereby destined to remain known forever. What they do not understand is that the freezer is the nearest human approximation to the Cloud of Unknowing: after three months, everything in it looks like everything else. The summer sun worked hard creating the distinctive goodnesses you freeze; don't let wintry oblivion hide them from you.

SIMPLE TOMATO SAUCE

2 cups frozen tomato purée
¼ cup butter
Salt and pepper to taste

Melt the purée over high heat, boil, remove from the heat, and stir in the butter till melted. Season to taste.

This is excellent just as it is; it's also a perfect base for sauces to which other ingredients will be added. Note, too, that it can be made either from peeled fresh tomatoes or — out of season — from canned tomatoes. Simply crush the tomatoes in their own juice and boil them down to the desired consistency before adding the butter.

ZUCCHINI FRITTATA

4 cups frozen, shredded zucchini (measured after squeezing
    out excess water)
4 eggs, beaten
1 cup grated Swiss, Muenster or Monterey Jack cheese
½ cup flour
½ teaspoon baking powder
½ cup chopped parsley
3 tablespoons chopped fresh (or 1 tablespoon dried) dill

Salt and pepper to taste
1 egg, beaten

Combine all ingredients except the last egg, and spoon into a buttered baking dish. Brush the remaining egg over the top and bake at 375° for 45 minutes or until the center has risen and the top is a golden brown. Cut into squares. *Serves 6.*

BARLEY, BEANS AND GREENS

BARLEY

1 medium onion, chopped
2 tablespoons butter
1 cup barley, washed
3 cups boiling stock (chicken, lamb, beef) or water
Salt to taste

Sauté the onion in the butter till soft but not browned, stir in barley, add stock, cover, and simmer until stock is absorbed.

BEANS

½ cup dried beans (marrow, navy, pea, lima, black-eyed
    peas — whatever), washed
Water to cover deeply
Salt to taste
Butter to taste

Combine the first 3 ingredients in a pot, boil for 1 minute, remove from the heat for an hour, then reboil, and simmer till just tender.

Drain and butter generously.

(Alternatively, heat up, say, canned black-eyed peas, drain, and butter.)

GREENS

¼ cup butter
1 small onion, chopped
2 cups frozen chopped greens

Sauté the onion in the butter till soft but not browned, add the greens, and heat through. Do not overcook: between the preliminary boiling and the freezing, they may need little or no additional cooking.

To serve, heat barley, beans and greens, and toss lightly together in a large bowl. Alternatively, put them out in separate bowls, and let guests combine them on their own plates. Serve with hot-pepper sauce. *Serves 4.*

While we're on the subject of freezing, however, here's another home-brew approach to consider.

By the time Labor Day rolls around each year, the summer's experience with preserving the fruits of the garden turns out to have added new wrinkles to the brain of the attentive cook. Old ways of doing the job have finally been recognized as flawed and better methods have taken up residence in the mind.

Consider, if you will, the preserving of herbs for winter use. For years, I doggedly *dried* my basil, coriander, marjoram, chervil, thyme, rosemary, tarragon and oregano. The authorities who favored this approach were of many opinions. Some insisted on air-drying only; others suggested artificial drying, either in a regular oven at the lowest setting or in a microwave. But by the end of the summer of '79, I had grown critical of the entire method.

Air-drying, admittedly, gave the best result; but what a poor best it was when compared with the fresh herbs themselves. Only the most robust of them — oregano, rosemary and thyme — came even close to keeping their fragrance. Tarragon lost some of its delightful anise overtones, and basil lost them all. Marjoram turned into something quite other; and coriander and chervil, like parsley, turned into nothing at all — unless you consider dried lawn clippings a fit addition to food.

About oven-drying, I had already come to a negative conclusion. The fragrances of herbs reside in certain highly volatile oils. On a 95° August day, a mere walk through the herb patch regales the nose with the symphony of essences that the sun is driving into the air right and left. What then was the point of cranking the heat up to 145° in a conventional oven, or up to 212° in a microwave? (Yes, Virginia, that's right. Microwaves work by boiling the water in food: they are not the cool customers they seem to be.)

Accordingly, I set out to develop some improved technology. If heat was the fragrance robber — and if air was the accomplice that carried off the loot — why not get rid of both of them? I might, of course, have put down my herbs in olive oil as some recommended. But I had smelled year-old olive oil many times in my career: why should I confuse the herbal issue with something that eventually would suggest only rancid paint?

That left freezing. But the techniques suggested by food writers left me, if not cold, then at least lukewarm. Some directed me to freeze them, chopped, in ice cubes. I declined. Why, having got rid of air that might waft away their bouquets, should I replace it with water to wash them away? Anyway, how accessible to the cook are leaves locked in ice? Other writers, of course, suggested freezing them as is. But they invariably did something silly in the process. They washed the herbs first: water still robbed them of their strength. So it was that I came to the Sausage Roll Method of Freezing Fresh Herbs.

It was simplicity itself. On the night before I harvested, I went to the garden and gently watered the herbs to remove sand. In the morning, after the sun had been up long enough to dry them off, but before it had pounded the fragrant daylights out of them, I picked. Then I brought them in, removed any tough stems, and stuffed them immediately into plastic bags: sandwich bags for small quantities, gallon bags for large ones. After that, all I did was push the herbs down tightly into each bag, roll it into a sausage shape, and enclose it in two more plastic bags, removing as much air as possible from each before tying it. Into the freezer, and the job was done.

The method's advantages were manifold. First, the herbs were instantly usable: I simply peeled back the plastic from the frozen roll of herbs, shaved off what I needed with a sharp knife, and returned the rest undamaged to the freezer. Second, with basil that I'd frozen this way, I was able to make pesto all winter. But third, there was the final astonishment of all: in February of '82, when I opened the last package of my "Basil 1980," suddenly it was summer all over again.

And with no airfare to Florida, at that.

8

When Not to Freeze

As a lesson, however, that not everything that *can* be done with a freezer *should* be done with a freezer, consider the following true, if slightly embroidered story.

The dinner was a party giver's nightmare. With deceptive smoothness, drinks and appetizers in the living room had paved the way for the evening's festivities, and it was an animated company that sat down, all expectation, at the table. The hostess smiled as she brought forth, in a lordly enameled dish, a steaming macédoine of lamb, baby carrots, white onions, lima beans, peas and sweet potatoes. Picking up her sterling serving spoons, she plunged them into the center of the casserole and paused dramatically to explain how she had prepared the mixture the day before and frozen it overnight.

She never got past her account of browning the lamb. Before she could mention so much as a single vegetable, the color drained from her face and the spoons fell from her hands. "Oh, no!" she groaned. "It's still frozen in the middle!" The cold was so intense it had transmitted itself up the solid silver handles at practically the speed of light.

Her guests, all solicitousness, suggested remedies. Plan A, to portion out warm first servings from the perimeter of the pan, was abandoned quickly. The steam that at first had risen so tantalizingly turned out to have been due mostly to the chill of the room: nowhere could a single cooked vegetable be found. Plan B, to accept humiliation and serve the dish anyway, was not even seriously considered. Since its principal advocate was the one person the hostess actively disliked, it was dismissed with a snappish "No, dear; we wouldn't want you breaking your dentures on a frozen carrot, would we?"

Plan C it was, then: her husband would serve the salad forthwith and she would return the offending dish to the oven. Thus, twenty impatient minutes and all the salad later — not to mention all the bread and the extra bottle of Château l'Angelus '67 — the casserole returned from the kitchen. But not, alas, from the limbo of half-baked ideas. If it was not now cold, neither yet was it cooked: hard slabs of sweet potato resisted the tooth; lukewarm, bulletlike limas fragmented in the mouth.

Dessert saved the evening: it was a chocolate torte of near-terminal richness followed by a bottle of Château Filhot '70. But there are less expensive ways of retrieving such culinary disasters. Let Plans D and E therefore be listed for the record.

Plan D is negative. A hostess should not freeze food she means to use the next day. Simple refrigeration is quite enough. Who but the lighting company benefits from saying to freezer and oven, "Let's you and him fight"?

Plan E, however, embodies a positive principle. The way to heat something through quickly is to stir it constantly over a hot *top burner*. Ovens take forever to cook the middle of a dish because the only things available to transmit heat to that point — carrots, say, or onions — are notoriously poor conductors. By contrast, setting a pan over high heat and stirring it frequently warms every particle of food directly.

Accordingly, the hostess in point should have *dismantled* her dish to heat it up. She should have borrowed a leaf from the cook who discovered, five minutes before a wedding luncheon was to be served, that a dish of chicken breasts Sandeman for forty was still cold. He simply poured off the sauce into one pan, put all the breasts into a second, turned up the heat under both and, when the sauce boiled, recombined the two. Service was hardly a minute late.

His reward, incidentally, was just the reverse of her punishment. As she lost one bottle of claret to a twenty-minute delay, so he gained six of champagne by denying his guests surplus time in which to consume them. He was, after all, not only the cook but the father of the bride.

9

Garnishes

"First impressions count!" we proclaim, trying to convince our children. Oddly, though, when it comes to food, we ourselves seem unconvinced. If we think at all of how a dish first presents itself to the eye of the beholder, we do so only the moment before the guests arrive. Surveying a well-cooked buffet supper, for example, we suddenly wish we'd paid more attention to appearances. The vast pan of baked ziti looks like nothing so much as a red, barren plain; the mountain of potato salad is of an unrelieved whiteness sufficient to cause snow-blindness. Where, we ask ourselves, are the *garnishes?* Oh, we lament, if only we were masters of more than the odd poke of parsley or the desperately scattered slice of egg.

True enough, with dishes as with people, looks aren't everything: the presence of garnishes can't make up for an absence of goodness. But it's just as great a mistake to think that good food is not helped by artful presentation. The garnishing of a dish proclaims the cook's care for both food and guests. "This is not just canned beans, friends," it says; "this is love in bloom."

Accordingly, to help you make almost any dish into a declaration of loving regard, here are step-by-step instructions for a good baker's dozen vegetable garnishes. As befits honest food, they are themselves all natural — no plastic daisies here; and, as is appropriate to the working cook, most of them are easily made. The only pieces of equipment needed are a sharp, thin paring knife, a sharp French chef's knife or its equivalent, a few bamboo skewers, and an old pair of chopsticks.

For a warmup, begin with that garniture of all work, the lowly, lovely lemon.

Lemon wedges. To make neat ones that don't show a lot of unsightly membrane, cut off both ends of the lemon so you can see where the membranes are. Then, standing the lemon on one of the cut ends, slice vertically through the middle of the flesh *between* two membranes. Trim the core off each wedge, flick out any seeds, and *voilà:* something better than mere hacked-up fruit.

Lemon crowns. Remove both ends of the lemon with parallel cuts and then cut the lemon in half crosswise. Notch the edge of the skin into V-shaped points all around the larger, cut surface of each half, taking out a bit of the flesh and removing any visible seeds as you go.

Notched lemon slices. Make a series of shallow parallel furrows down the length of the lemon (removing V-shaped strips of skin) until you have scored meridians of longitude around the whole. Cut into thin slices crosswise and flick out seeds.

For something ever so slightly more elaborate, try scallion flowers and, by extension, leek or long pepper flowers.

Scallion flowers. Trim medium-thick scallions, cutting off the roots, removing wilted outer leaves and cutting off most, but not all of the green, leaving yourself with 3-to-4-inch pieces of scallion.

Lay each piece on its side and, beginning about 1 inch from the bottom end, make a series of parallel lengthwise cuts with the point of a paring knife, rolling the scallion a little each

time before starting a new cut. (There are several ways of doing this: perhaps the fastest is to hold the knife like a pencil,
with your middle finger almost all the way down at the tip so
that it can function as a depth gauge for the cuts.)

Put the finished "flowers" in cold water and refrigerate 24
hours, or at least overnight. They will curl gorgeously.

Leek and *long pepper flowers*. Obviously, a large leek will
make a monster blossom and, perhaps less obviously, so will
long peppers (Italian frying peppers, cayenne peppers, and so
forth). For these last, simply make longitudinal cuts from
near the stem end all the way through the tip, get the seeds and
membranes out as best you can, and refrigerate under water
for 24 hours.

Next, for some of the best-looking vegetable flowers of all, try
tomato roses, grapefruit, orange or even lemon roses, and cherry
tomato buds.

Tomato roses. Take a firm red tomato (the gas-ripened
jobs in the supermarket, so useless for any other purpose, are
perfect for this). Beginning at the blossom, or smooth end, make
a flat cut parallel to the top of the tomato. This cut should produce a "tab" of tomato skin about ⅛ inch thick and/or 1 to 1½
inches in diameter. Do not, however, cut the tab off: instead,
segue from a slicing to a peeling motion and peel off the entire
skin of the tomato in a single, unbroken band about 1 inch wide.

Don't make the band of peel either too thick (that makes
it hard to roll up later on) or too thin (that invites breaks). On
the other hand, do try to vary the *width* of the band as much as
possible (it's just those ups and downs that give the best impression of petals).

Lay out the band of peel, skin side up, on a clean towel
and, beginning with the end at which you finished cutting, roll
the entire skin up in a fairly tight curl. When you reach the
tab you first made, look at the curl, decide which end looks more

like a rose, and rest the whole curl, other end down, on the tab. When well made, tomato roses will hold their shape without further fastening. They can be used immediately, but they will keep nicely in the refrigerator if you cover them with paper toweling soaked in cold water.

Grapefruit, orange and lemon roses. Same procedure; just be sure to use fairly thin-skinned fruit and to peel it thinly enough to obviate its cracking when rolled up. Also (particularly with grapefruit, which otherwise makes a boring flower), be *sure* to vary the width of the band of peel as dramatically as you can. Finally, a toothpick may be needed to keep citrus roses from unraveling.

Cherry tomato buds. Set two parallel bamboo skewers 1 inch apart on the cutting board and put the cherry tomato between them, stem end down. Keeping the blade of the knife pointing straight across the skewers at all times, make two slightly angled-in downward cuts, one on either side of the center of the tomato. These cuts should remove a small V-shaped segment whose narrow edge occurs at the point where the knife meets the skewers. Rotate the tomato 90 degrees on its vertical axis and repeat. Remove the bits and pieces, leaving four "petals." Pipe a bit of mayonnaise in the center of each flower, or use a bit of carrot or hard-boiled-egg yolk for a center.

The use of skewers brings us to another trick of cutting, this time with chopsticks.

Chrysanthemum turnip. Lay a good-size white turnip on its side, and remove the ends with parallel cuts at least 1½ to 2 inches apart. Stand the center section on one end, and trim it neatly into the largest possible straight-sided cylinder you can produce.

Stand this cylinder upright on the cutting board between two parallel chopsticks and, beginning at one side, make a series of precisely parallel vertical cuts across the entire top of the cylinder. These cuts should be $\frac{1}{16}$ inch apart and go all the way down to the chopsticks. Then, rotating the cylinder 90 degrees on its vertical axis, repeat the process.

Place the now cross-hatched cylinder cut side up in a small dish, sprinkle the top with $\frac{1}{2}$ teaspoon salt, and allow to stand for 20 minutes.

Gently squeeze the excess moisture out of the turnip, set it cut side up once again in the dish, and pour over it some white vinegar sweetened to taste with sugar.

When you are ready to use it, form the turnip into a chrysanthemum by spreading out the "petals." Alternatively, if the turnip is large, you can break it into three or four pieces at its base and form each piece into a smaller chrysanthemum. In either case, put something by way of a focal point in the center of each flower — a bit of red pepper, some poppy seeds or some black sesame seeds.

Next, for a variation of the chopstick gambit, try turning out bell pepper cups for mayonnaise, mustard, tartare sauce, ketchup, and other dressings.

Bell pepper cups. Take a large, regularly formed bell pepper and trim the stem end so that it will stand upright (but do not either make openings into the cavity or remove the part of the stem in the pepper itself). Then, standing the pepper upright, put parallel wooden stop blocks on either side of it. (These will function exactly as the chopsticks did, but should be high enough to stop the knife about halfway down the pepper; two cookbooks of appropriate and equal height will serve in an emergency. Then make a series of parallel vertical cuts as you did for the turnip (this time making them a good $\frac{1}{8}$ inch apart), followed, as before, by a second series at right angles to the first.

Pick out the bits and pieces, remove seeds and membranes, and refrigerate the resulting cup in cold water for 24 hours.

❋

Last but not least, the humble but abundant carrot flower.

Carrot flowers. Take a straight, large, unpeeled carrot and let it stand outside the refrigerator for a day or two — or until it becomes a bit rubbery. (Crisp, firm carrots are hard to work with.)

With a paring knife, shape the lower end into a perfectly regular, long, four-sided pyramidal point. Then, setting the knife on the peel just above one of the flat sides of this pyramid, slice down toward the point, cutting as close to the surface as possible, but not going all the way to the point. (Once you get the knack of this, you will automatically end the cut by drawing the knife back and letting the point cut toward the center of the carrot. This helps in the final twisting off of the flower.)

Repeat this same cut on the other three sides of the pyramid and gently twist the four-petaled flower free. Drop it into cold water, true up the end of the carrot into a proper pyramid once more, and begin another flower. One long carrot, deftly dealt with, will produce dozens.

But for a thirteenth garnish more abundant than them all, take a 3-to-4-inch length of large carrot and cut longitudinal notches in it to produce a pleasing cross-sectional shape (a star, perhaps, or a maple leaf — be creative). Then slice it paper-thin crosswise, and store the slices in cold water till needed. After even a relatively short bath, these sprinkle-about accents acquire unpredictable and charming twists.

There! As long as you don't garnish all your dishes dead center — or bury them under so many flowers they look like a gangster's funeral — you are well on your way to making the desert of unadorned dishes blossom like the rose.

10

More Than a Garnish

If you were told of a slim, lovely creature, assertive but not overbearing, yet modest without being mousy, would you not expect to find that her date book was full, and that offers of marriage were a dime a dozen? But if you learned this was far from the case — that in fact she was considered a fit partner only for picnics and cold suppers, and that all the proposals for important occasions and lifelong associations were made to her fat, ugly sisters instead — what would you think? Would you not conclude that an injustice was being done? Would you not try to shake some sense into her suitors?

Well, you do know such a creature: the scallion, a vegetable whose excellences find no room in most cooks' hearts or kitchens, but that hardly deserves such gross neglect. It is commonly used in one way only: raw, to be dipped in salt. But how unfair! To take one of the milder members of the onion family and serve it so that it gets more blame than any of them for producing dragon breath! To forbear incorporating it into other dishes! To fail even to try serving it cooked by itself! Sad, sad, sad.

But luckily, not irremediable. Take, to begin with, the case of scallions solo. If leeks, their gargantuan cousins, can be poached lightly in salted water and then marinated in a suitable

vinaigrette, why not these more manageable delicacies? Cut
into, say, 1¼-inch lengths — up to and including the beginning
of the green part — and arranged nicely on a small plate of leaf
lettuce with some of the vinaigrette poured over, two or three
bunches of scallions will make a fine first course for four. And
obviously there is nothing to prevent you from padding them
out with similarly poached asparagus, green beans, or whatever
else may be in season.

Which brings up the next remedy. Scallions are the sovereign stretcher of vegetables in short supply. Did your spinach
practically disappear in the cooking? Never mind. Simply chop
a bunch or two of scallions into short lengths, stir-fry them
briefly in butter, then add the spinach and heat it through. Have
you no veggies in the house but a few minuscule zucchini and
a half a head of lettuce? Small matter. Slice them up as you
like, add a bunch of scallions, appropriately cut, and stir-fry
everything lightly in butter or olive oil. Behold, a vegetable dish
worthy of the best of company!

There is more, though. Scallions are better at barbecues
than onions could ever hope to be, especially with skewered
meats. Putting whole onions between chunks of beef simply
pushes the pieces apart, precludes any important transfer of
tastes and practically guarantees the onions will be underdone
when the beef is overcooked. And sliced onions? Well . . . who
has not watched them come unstuck and hang like sagging loops
below the meat? But skewering with scallions? Ah! The skewer
pierces the scallion from the side, holding it permanently in
place; and the next piece of meat snuggles tightly against both
it and the previous piece, absorbing flavor and preventing drying out.

Finally, there are chopped scallions. For this purpose use
the whole stalk, green and all. Indeed, if you simply trim your
scallions when you bring them home from the market and store
them in a plastic bag, they will keep for over a week and pro-

vide you with instantly choppable onion for any purpose — for inclusion in dishes to be cooked, such as croquettes, casseroles, home fries and potato cakes, where they add color as well as flavor; and for sprinkling on top of dishes about to be served, such as mashed potatoes, Chinese foods and the like.

The scallion, in short, is no mere party girl. It's a wise cook who takes her home to meet the family.

11

Salt

"Protect yourself against killer salt," runs the catalog caption. For a mere $99 plus freight, you can be the proud owner of the Original Salt Meter. Simply plug it into the nearest wall outlet (in your hostess's dining room, perhaps?), insert the probe into any liquid or solid food (her *billi bi?* her artfully arranged *pâté de campagne?* her *salade niçoise?*) and the meter will "electronically calibrate what the salt-range is: high; moderate; low." And, in all likelihood, your own social-acceptability range: low; submarginal; abysmal. *O tempora! O mores!* Oh, well.

In the name of fairness, it should be said that the catalog flackery for this device does not suggest taking it to dinner parties. Rather, it limits the recommended uses to monitoring the "sodium levels in canned foods, juices, strained baby foods, frozen and fast foods." But in the name of plain horse sense, the current outcry against salt as "a new villain" still needs a good three-fourths of the wind let out of it.

No doubt the whole campaign — and the profusion of others just like it — was inevitable. The human race, unable or unwilling to accept responsibility for its countless contributions to the danger of living, seems to find comfort in shifting the blame onto lower orders of creation. Sugar, fiber, starch and fat, seared chicken, rare beef, raw fish and live clams have all been pilloried as threats. How sad, though, that out of all the long procession of innocents we have thus fitted for black hats, we now find it necessary to revile one that is a true friend. If we keep it up, we will find ourselves on speaking terms with nothing but dirt, water and turnip greens.

If that. This penchant for discrediting the dietary wisdom of the race is not, for all its scientific trappings, a nice habit. Oh, yes, there's a skin of reason on it: there are, quite plainly, people with exceptional physiologies who must not eat this or that; there are obviously certain things that no one should eat at all; and there is certainly no earthly substance that is not liable to misapplication or abuse. But what a thin, elementary skin it is, and what a volume of mean-spirited hot air it encompasses. All too often it is a cloak for dispositions that would rather borrow trouble than behold goodness — that relish theoretical bogeymen more than any real creature in this grandly material world.

Consider salt, then. Without it we would not only have difficulty being well, we would not be here at all: all life came from the salt sea. And all our history has been salted as well. Salt's preservative qualities made it a symbol of enduring compacts (the Old Testament records a "covenant of salt"); its necessity in climates without ice made it precious (salt was offered in sacrifices to God); its preciousness made it a measure of labor (he who earns a *salary* is worth his *salt*); its sovereign use as a seasoning — to sharpen and define, give balance and point to the taste of food — made it the perfect metaphor for all that is piquant in life (a salty character, a salacious dance); and to think of life without it was the very antithesis of wisdom (if salt "loses its savor," it becomes, literally, foolish — in Greek, the phrase is *mōranthē*).

There is no denying, of course, that salt can be overused at both stove and table. Like the habit of raising one's voice, it can be addictive — the previous overdose becoming not just an isolated excess but a baseline for further excesses still. Cooking with too much salt is like insisting on a loud piccolo part in every orchestral piece: it turns what should have been a seasoning into the dominant feature of the composition. Eating a meal that has had salt poured over everything on the plate is like reading a book with too many exclamation points: the punctuation becomes the message.

Yet to cook without salt (save for sound and personal medical reasons), or to deliberately undersalt in the name of dietary chic, is to omit from the music of cookery the indispensable bass line over which all other tastes and smells form their harmonies. For example, it is a common fault of otherwise excellent Italian pastries that their sweetness wanders vaguely over the palate. Why? They lack the grounding that just a pinch of salt can give. Indeed, just as tasters add to tea a few drops of skim milk as a point of reference for their faculties, so there is hardly a cook in the world worth his or her . . . Lapsang Souchong, shall we say . . . who does not ask of every dish, "Is the salt correct?" — who does not, in short, relate its riot of aromas and flavors to a judicious salinity that reconciles and governs them all.

To the barricades, then, for salt! Down with this trendy blaming of substances when the problem lies obviously in the dose! Off with these meter-toting alarmists who discover evils under every culinary bed! Out with their stigmatizing of salt as sodium and letting it go at that! No mere metallic element shaped our history; no dull chemical formula salted our speech with images. It was a great, necessary, simple, lip-smacking *taste* that got us where we are: *Don't let them take it away!*

12

The Compleat Leftoeuvrière

No refreshing of the roots of cookery can be complete, however, unless one further, major subject is addressed. It is all well and good to speak of fundamentals like invention and improvisation, to praise the power of the unaided hand and to strike a blow for salt. But without a word about the vast, all-encompassing culinary realm in which they come together every day, we fall far short. Permit me, therefore, a suitably biblical introduction to so central a matter.

There be three things which the long days cannot preclude, yea, four which summer's heat causeth to flourish: a refrigerator with more food after dinner than before; cooked pasta in countless shapes but short supply; the scrap of steak that sitteth solitary in plastic wrap; and company that arriveth unannounced.

Put them all together and they spell Leftover Cookery: to some a curse, but to those with the wisdom to resist vain repetition, a sovereign deliverance from the bondage of recipes into the freedom of invention. God does nothing twice. He makes no two snowflakes alike and never sends the same high tide again. And man, in his image, goes ill unless he goes with the flow of change: only fools try to repeat a party; any gravy that is not doctored the second time around becomes inexorably worse.

Therefore the first principle in the use of leftovers is that their service is a branch of cookery, not of reheatery, micro-wavery or thin-slicery. Cold *Spätzle* need more than warming: they need extra nutmeg. Yesterday's *suprême de volaille* cries for fresh pepper. Last night's ratatouille has lost the savor of its salt. The cook who leads leftovers only from cold to hot leads them nowhere but down the compost-bin path.

But more fundamental than even that principle is the need for character on the part of the cook. "Know thyself," said the ancient Greek proverb; the modern householder, too, must look long and long at unquestioned saving ways. This cold linguine you so diligently bag and tie: will you really use it, or are you only waiting for blue mold to absolve you of the guilt of wasting food? These halves of baked potato you squirrel away in foil: will they actually see the inside of a frying pan, or will they simply languish until, brown of edge and cracked of face, they are fit for nothing but the void? This four-sevenths of a portion of lamb and gravy you freeze: dare you ask yourself why? To be sure, a full freezer is more economical than an empty one. But full of what? Of unwept, unhonored and unidentifiable *rocks?* Of food that, when finally thawed, will have not only the age but the appeal of mastodon stew?

One third of all the leavings you refrigerate — and three-fourths of all the scraps you freeze — should have been tossed to the beagles to begin with. It's cooks who lead unexamined lives who give leftovers a bad name. Repent, therefore: save only what you know you will use; use promptly everything you save; and behold, the kingdom of leftover cookery will be at hand.

In that happy realm — so unlike this despotic world of zoning laws, financial aid forms and IRS regulations — there are only two rules and one corollary. First, change the seasonings of any food you serve twice. Second, change its state. And the corollary: whenever possible, change both.

Change of seasoning. All leftovers, excepting only desserts, profit by the addition of sautéed onion. No gravy is worsened by Madeira. A handful of fresh herbs revives even the most moribund tomato sauce. Cold pasta, no matter what else you do with it, takes kindly to Pepper Oil, Basil Oil, or both.

You do not know these oils? Permit me to introduce you.

Take two clean mustard jars. Stuff one with coarsely chopped fresh hot peppers and the other with minced fresh basil leaves and garlic. Fill the jars with olive oil and let them stand, covered but unrefrigerated, for a few hours, days or weeks. To use, simply dip a table knife into the jar and allow the oil it takes up to run off onto the food. Store on the table, but sprinkle indiscriminately everywhere. There are only nine substances in the world that are not improved by these oils, and most people go to their reward without discovering more than three.

Change of state. Cold spaghetti should be fried crisp in butter, then half-softened in sauce. Result? New taste, new texture, new dish. Cold boiled potatoes can be quartered, sixthed, or eighthed and deep-fried in oil. Product? Free cottage fries, or whatever fries a steak house would have the nerve to charge you for. Cold rice simply begs to become rice pudding.

You would like a recipe? Allow me to correct a misapprehension.

Rice pudding is a habit, not a recipe. The practiced *left-oeuvrière* does not intellectualize when she adds sugar, grated lemon rind, milk and vanilla to her tired rice. She just boils it long enough to make it look right and adds more of everything till it tastes good.

Which brings us, logically, to the corollary. For if rice pudding is a mere behavior pattern, the farther reaches of second-day cookery are habits that transcend themselves and become positive virtues.

Take salads made of leftovers, for example. The habit is nothing more than the reflex action of mixing cold, chopped anything with diced celery and mayonnaise. The virtue arises from being willing to use whatever is at hand and from knowing which seasonings will best enhance it. Was it leftover roast beef or steak? Add dry mustard and Worcestershire. Was it lamb? Try curry powder. Did you cube three pork chops? Why not fresh chervil or sage? Chicken? How about tarragon? Fish? Mace or green peppercorns, perhaps?

Or, to give but one more instance, consider this further variation on Fannie Farmer's protean wonder, Denver Chocolate Pudding. Butter a 9-by-9-inch baking dish. In the bottom, put a layer of diced meat, fish, or vegetable, accented judiciously with chopped onion, celery, green pepper, cheese or what-have-you. Over that, spread a layer of prepared biscuit mix (2 cups mix, ⅔ cup milk). Over that, pour a leftover sauce that you have stretched with heavy cream to 1½ cups and then seasoned inventively. Bake 40 minutes at 350°: the sauce will go underneath as the biscuit comes up, this time giving you bread, meat, and gravy, all in one dish fit for six kings or four teenage princes.

And, of course, for the chef, who in addition enjoys the liberation of leftover cookery. Like God, who made the world out of nothing, the cook who creates from cold scratch need produce only *something* — *anything* — and he is beyond the reach of failure. Indeed he may, unless he disciplines himself, imitate the divine largesse more closely than he intended. Leftover leftovers are alarmingly possible. Like the knife that has been in the family for a hundred years — and that has had three new blades and five new handles in the same century — there are dishes that can lose their identity a dozen times and never once imperil their existence.

In part, therefore, as a paradigm of that constant danger (once, after six reincarnations of the dish that follows, I still threw out enough to cover half the back yard), but principally as an inspiration to let nothing you dismay — not even the most cluttered beach-house refrigerator — I give you the great-granddaddy of all *leftoeuvres*.

Admittedly, the specifications for this concoction sound like a spoof. Nevertheless, it is a perfectly respectable dish: indeed, in the hands of a cook who knows how to make a prudent selection of ingredients, it can even transcend its mongrel origins and become a thoroughbred. But be careful. It smothers grass as well as weeds.

SUMMER COTTAGE CLOSEOUT

or How to Empty a Fire Island Larder After Four Weeks' Vacation

1. Take all the cold pasta you can find. If it's chunky, leave it alone; if it's long, run a knife through it a few times; if it's not enough, cook more (using up half-empty boxes first, but remembering the desirability of self-restraint). Put all the pasta in a huge bowl. Better yet, put it in a 20-quart pot.

2. Take all the leftover meats, cheese and vegetables you have on hand: beef, lamb, pork, veal, chicken, duck, turkey, goose, hot dogs, hamburgers, sausages, kielbasa, bologna, bacon, salami, pepperoni, mozzarella, Swiss, Muenster, Cheddar, Romano, blue, Stilton, Gorgonzola, broccoli, beans, peas, mushrooms — and cut them into bite-size pieces. Add to the pot.

3. Put some olive oil in a frying pan and lightly sauté plenty of chopped onion and garlic in it. (If you have uncooked bacon, ground meat or sausage, fry that before you do the onions.) Add all this, too, to the pot.

4. Take whatever leftover tomato sauces and meat gravies you may have and stir them in, along with judicious admixtures of any or all of the following, until the whole is very wet indeed: fresh or canned tomatoes (peeled and crushed with their juice), tomato purée, wine (red, white or fortified), sweet cream, sour

cream, cottage cheese, ricotta, plain yogurt, milk, chicken stock, beef broth. (If, in the end, the color seems to have wandered off the spectrum, add tomato paste until you feel better about it.) Mix everything once again.

5. Season with salt, black pepper, grated cheese and lots of herbs — basil, thyme, marjoram, rosemary, tarragon, sage, savory, chive. Add red pepper and mix again.

6. Go back to *Step 4* and make it all wetter.

7. Go back to *Step 5* and season it all again.

8. Mix well and pour the contents of the pot into an aluminum dinghy — or, lacking that, into the largest baking vessel your oven will hold. Give it 1 to 2 hours at 375°. Serve hot — and go for a walk on the beach when it comes time to decide what to do with the remains.

On second thought, I cannot leave the subject of *leftoeuvrage* with such a wide-angle shot. For something more tightly focused, try

ZWIEBELFLEISCH

2 cups sliced onions
¼ cup butter
6 medium-thick slices leftover sauerbraten or pot roast
1 cup cold leftover gravy
½ pound Cheddar, Emmenthaler or Gruyère cheese, shredded
 coarse

Sauté the onions in the butter, uncovered, until golden brown.

Arrange the slices of meat on a baking sheet, leaving spaces between them. Top each one with cold gravy, sautéed onion and grated cheese, and bake at 400° till the cheese melts and browns slightly.

Serve with leftover *Kartoffelklösse* (potato dumplings) that have been sliced in half and sautéed in butter — and, of course, with leftover red cabbage, if you have any. *Serves 6.*

PART II

Branching Out Through the Seasons

13

A German Christmas Eve

Oddly, my fondest recollections of Christmas Eve come from across the street. Not that there weren't lots of presents at my own house. And not that I didn't look forward to my mother's Christmas dinner. I was, in fact, inordinately proud that we had a standing rib roast and Yorkshire pudding while the rest of the block was gnawing its way through vulcanized turkeys. It was just that by the time I was in my early teens, the Englishness of my native household had induced in me a deep impatience with all the waiting that went on.

Our holidays went strictly by the clock. You couldn't have your stocking presents till you woke up on Christmas morning. Then you had to wait for everyone else to appear in bathrobes for the opening of major under-the-tree presents. Next you waited for grandparents and dinner at one. After that, it was tap your toe through dessert, cordials and dishes till everyone reassembled for the next round of presents. And then there was always the concluding opening session, to be triggered only by the arrival of stray aunts and uncles who, having promised to show at five, never appeared till six at the earliest.

But across the street was another world. My friend Arthur's

family were German. Their entire celebration was compressed
into one glorious orgy of gifts and goodies on Christmas Eve. I
think I was thirteen when I cadged my first invitation out of his
mother, my Aunt Lotte (those were the days when well-bred
children did not call adults by their first names, and so acquired
large clutches of Dutch aunts and uncles). In any case, she took
pity on me for the strictness of my upbringing and, after I
started going to Midnight Mass, put off her own Christmas Eve
festivities till church was over and I was free to take part.

Talk about the theology of liberation! It had always struck
me as strange that we would celebrate the birth of a Deliverer
and then do nothing with our professed enthusiasm except go
home and sleep it off. Imagine, therefore, my delight when I
found that straight across from me and two houses down were
people who apparently never went to bed at all — and who
brooked not one of the dull delays with which my own Christ-
mases were encrusted.

We would hit Tante Löttchen's at about 12:45. Uncle Emil
and Uncle Otto had long ago begun and by then were pressing
beer on anyone over three feet tall, and their attentions on all
females over twelve. They were not exactly a moralist's cup of
tea, I suppose; but then neither was the friend of publicans and
sinners whose nativity they were whooping up.

That initial theological insight was vouchsafed in the
kitchen, just off the side door. (Tante Löttchen's front door had,
I think, rusted shut; at any rate, the house's only customary en-
trance landed you right between the stove and the table.) It
was when you got to the dining room, though, that the second
and profounder revelation occurred. I am sure I remember only
half of it, but there, on the all but obscured table, was the whole
feast at once; steaming plates of weisswurst, knackwurst and
bauernwurst; great bowls of sauerkraut with caraway, bean
salad with onions, and potato salad with bacon; wursts as nu-
merous as the stars in the sky — plockwurst, gelbwurst, speck-
wurst, braunschweiger, kassler leberwurst, onion leberwurst,

blutwurst, tirolerwurst, ham bologna, landjaeger and touristen-
wurst; pickled herring, creamed herring, rollmops and brathe-
ringe; and mustards, butter and four kinds of pumpernickel.
Better yet, nobody waited for anything, not even grace — on
the sound theological principle, as I now see it, that there is no
piety in holding up a celebration when God has announced he's
not waiting for us to be pious. If grace visits us in our sins, it's
ungracious not to start cheering right away.

But best of all, dessert was on the table from the start.
None of that English restraint by which the roast had to be
cleared before the plum pudding was lit; just apfelkuchen and
pitchers of heavy cream, and dig in whenever you liked.

When did the presents come? They never *didn't* come.
People swapped them on the way in, opened them all over the
place, even on top of the *kartoffelsalat,* and went on doing so
all through the festivities. There was a timetable of sorts for
the most important gifts — Tante's and the smallest children's
— but it was set by no clock. They were given out when Uncle
Emil, having progressed from three to four sheets to the wind,
finally got into his Santa Claus suit and passed them around.

Many years later, reading a collection of medieval Latin
verse, I came across a poem about a man who had been to
heaven and came back with a report that Saint Peter was the
Head Cook. The poet had in mind, of course, to take a dim
view of the claim. But after those Christmas Eves at Tante
Löttchen's, I'm not so sure the man who went to heaven wasn't
on the right track: Saint Peter, if he's pictured in the poet's way
as a Gatekeeper with a great, grim ring of keys, looks more like
law than grace. In fact, he looks exactly like the fuzz.

If I ever put up my own statue of the Prince of the Apos-
tles, he will be short and round like my Tante Löttchen, and for
the symbols of his authority, he will have, not keys on his belt,
but a string of sausages around his neck: down with Yale &
Towne; up with Schaller & Weber. And three cheers for the
grace that wouldn't wait.

14

A Holiday Smörgåsbord

Chhristmas holidays! The words instantly conjure up a vision of the overfull date book: on Sunday at four, eggnog and cookies at the Harringtons; on Tuesday at five, rum punch and fruitcake with the Smiths; on Wednesday, cocktails and cheese with Sam and Jerry; on Thursday ... But why continue? The case for what is amiss practically makes itself.

Note first, though, what is *not* wrong with this frenzy of celebration. It is not that too much time is spent gadding about: if God visited and redeemed his people, we do ill if we do not celebrate with some visiting of our own. Nor is it that we are too unspiritual: if God took humanity seriously enough to come into it the same way we do, and in the back of a barn at that, it seems fairly plain that the secular is even more his cup of tea than the sacred. And it is not the presence of so much of the grape, the barleycorn and the sugar cane: if, years afterward, the son of Mary provided a hundred and thirty gallons of wine for a wedding reception already well on the way, there would seem to be no cosmic objection to spiritous holidays.

No. What is wrong is not the presence in our festivities of too much that is material, but the absence from them of food that matters sufficiently. Our mistake is to have acquiesced in the cocktail party as the paradigm of Christmas celebration: the Word who became flesh can scarcely have had it in mind for us to commemorate his coming by standing on one foot and munching stuffed mushrooms, *crudités* and miniature quiches. The holidays cry out for food as material as the festival: serious food for serious consumption by serious eaters — all in the name of a serious banishing of chic solemnity from our midst.

Without further introduction, therefore, consider the smörgåsbord. Admittedly, it's a bit of work — several days' worth of bits, if you come right down to it. But to anyone for whom cooking is an act of provident love and not just a minimum effort aimed at maximum social pay-back, it is the holiday entertainment par excellence.

What is presented here, however, is not the usual smörgåsbord manqué — not the polyglot, wedding-palace buffet of baked lasagne, chopped liver, Greek olives and Chinese spareribs; nor yet the catch-as-catch-can, everybody-bring-a-noodle-pudding church supper — rather, it is the only smörgåsbord with a clear title to the name: the genuine Swedish article, produced under the supervision of a single dedicated cook.

True enough, its relentlessly Scandinavian bill of fare may strike some as strange: it *does* have rather a lot of herring in it, not to mention anchovies and some raw-meat-and-egg delicacies that delicate eaters may pass up. But there are more than enough other items to please the non-Vikings in the crowd: meat balls, head cheese, savory potatoes and Paris snacks (or, to give them an authentic ring, *köttbollar, kalvsylta, Janssons Frestelse* and *Parisiersmörgåsar*), plus brown beans, pickled beets, old man's hash, knäckebröd, Swedish cheeses — and, for dessert, the almond tart called Mazarin cake.

Served with freezing cold *akvavit* and plenty of beer, this menu cannot fail to turn any holiday gathering into that glorious company of concelebrants that cocktail parties only pretend to create. At those dismal, sip-and-nibble gatherings, people spend hours cruising the house in search of the action that all evening eludes them. At a true smörgåsbord, from the moment the first herring goes on the buffet to the time, often hours later, when the last hot specialty comes out of the oven, there is never a minute's doubt where the action is: it is on, at, over, and perhaps even under, the groaning, all but blanketed board.

A toast to the smörgåsbord, then: may it make your Christmas, your guests and yourself *matter* supremely. "Min skål, din skål, alla vackra flickors skål" — which, roughly translated, means either, "Malt doth more than Milton can to reconcile God's ways to man," or else, "Make me a youth again, just for tonight." In any case, Happy Holidays.

A word about ingredients and availability before going on to the recipes.

1. Swedish anchovies (*Ansjovis Sprats*). These are available in specialty stores and many delicatessens. They are canned in a sweet, spiced sauce — often called lobster sauce (*hummersås*) — and they bear almost no resemblance to Mediterranean anchovies, which cannot be substituted for them. They also come packed either whole (requiring boning and skinning for most dishes), or already filleted. They are essential to an authentic smörgåsbord.

2. Pickled herring (*Inlagdsill*). Canned, already pickled herring fillets in dill sauce, wine sauce, and so forth are available in specialty shops. However, unprepared headless herrings are also available — the commonest being the salted Holland herrings packed in five-pound plastic barrels (one barrel is enough for a large party). When shopping for these last fish, be sure to look for a barrel marked "mixed" — containing both males and females — otherwise you will not get the roe

necessary for one of the best dishes of all, Mock Oyster Pudding.

3. Brown beans (*Bruna Bönor*). Swedish brown beans can be bought in specialty stores, as can golden syrup. In a pinch, however, red kidney beans and dark Karo syrup can be substituted.

4. As for serving the smörgåsbord, obviously it is possible to set out large plates and serve all the dishes at once. But since Americans tend to fill their plates with everything on the table at the same time, and since that invariably results in an omnium-gatherum of a dish that makes a mishmash of distinctive flavors, it's best to put out small plates and serve the cold items before bringing on the hot ones.

5. The recipes for the smörgåsbord that follow will serve 20 to 30 persons.

PICKLED HERRING THREE WAYS

I. IN WINE SAUCE

½ cup white wine
½ cup vinegar
¼ cup sugar (or more, to taste)
2 tablespoons pickling spice
1 tablespoon white peppercorns
1 small onion, sliced
6 to 8 herring fillets (the whole salt herrings having first been soaked for 12 hours in several changes of cold water before boning and skinning)

Bring the first six ingredients to a boil. Remove from the heat and cool completely.

Put the herring fillets in a suitable shallow dish, strain the pickling liquid over them, and marinate overnight in the refrigerator. Cut into bite-size pieces before serving.

II. IN DILL SAUCE

½ cup white wine
½ cup vinegar
⅓ cup sugar (or more, to taste)
3 tablespoons dill weed (or to taste)
6 to 8 salt herring fillets (as above)

Bring the first four ingredients to a boil. Remove from the heat and cool completely.

Put the herring fillets in a suitable dish, pour the unstrained pickling liquid over them, and marinate overnight in the refrigerator. Cut into bite-size pieces before serving.

III. IN SOUR CREAM

6 to 8 pickled herring fillets, fully prepared as in I, above
1 cup sour cream
⅓ cup strained pickling liquid (from I, above)
2 medium onions (or more), sliced thin

Cut the herring fillets into bite-size pieces, mix everything together, and refrigerate till needed.

HERRING SALAD

SALAD

6 to 8 herring fillets pickled in dill sauce, diced
¼ cup vinegar
½ teaspoon white pepper
1 to 2 tablespoons sugar
1 cup cooked beef, veal, lamb or pork, diced
1 cup cooked beets, diced
1 cup cooked potatoes, diced
2 sweet gherkins, diced
2 peeled, cored apples, diced

GARNISH

Unsweetened, lightly salted whipped cream (or mayonnaise
delicately colored with beet juice)
Sliced hard-boiled eggs, stuffed tomatoes, parsley, etc.

Mix the nine salad ingredients thoroughly, pack into a fish mold
(or other suitable mold) that has been rinsed out with cold
water, and refrigerate. Unmold the salad onto a platter, mask
with whipped cream or mayonnaise, and decorate with sliced
eggs and other garnishes.

ANCHOVY EYE

6 to 8 Swedish anchovy fillets, chopped fine
1 raw egg yolk
1 medium onion, chopped fine

Arrange the chopped anchovy in a circular mound in the center of a small plate, make a well in the middle of it, and carefully slip the egg yolk into the well. Arrange the chopped onion
around the outside of the anchovy so that it has the shape of
the white of an eye.

The first guest to tackle this dish gets the privilege of mixing it all up.

SWEDISH STEAK TARTARE

1 pound best-quality lean beef, chopped fine
¼ cup capers, chopped
Salt and white pepper to taste
1 raw egg yolk
2 medium-size cold boiled potatoes, cut into small dice
2 medium-size cooked beets, cut into small dice
¼ cup chopped red onion

Mix the first three ingredients together and arrange in a flat round in the center of a serving plate. Score a pleasing pattern on it with the back of a knife blade, make a well in the middle, and slip the yolk into the well. Garnish the edge of the plate attractively with the remaining three ingredients. Serve with buttered *knäckebröd*.

KALVSYLTA
(Swedish Jellied Veal)

2 pounds neck of veal
1 veal knuckle
Water to cover
Salt to taste (lightly, at first)
½ teaspoon white pepper
2 tablespoons vinegar (or to taste)
1 teaspoon powdered plain gelatine, softened in 1 tablespoon cold water (use more gelatine if you want a very firm result)

Simmer the first four ingredients for 2 to 3 hours, or until very tender. Take out the meat, remove bones and sinews, and let the stock boil hard while you cut the meat into small pieces. Strain the stock, add the meat, pepper, and vinegar, correct the seasoning, and add the gelatine. Cool for 10 minutes, pour into a suitable mold, and refrigerate overnight.

Cut into slices, arrange them on a platter, and garnish with pickled beets.

PICKLED BEETS

⅔ cup vinegar
½ cup beet juice
1 cup sugar (or more, to taste)
Salt to taste
2 tablespoons pickling spice
2 cans beets, sliced thin
2 medium onions, sliced into rings

Bring the first five ingredients to a boil. Put the sliced beets in a bowl, and strain the pickling liquid over them. Refrigerate overnight.

Add the onion 1 hour before serving.

SWEDISH BROWN BEANS

This can be prepared the day before.

2 cups Swedish brown beans or red kidney beans (alternatively, canned red kidney beans can be used to avoid the preliminary cooking)
5 cups water
Salt to taste
¼ cup golden syrup, or to taste (dark Karo syrup can be substituted)
¼ cup vinegar, or to taste

If using dry beans, rinse them, add water and salt, and simmer until tender (1 to 2 hours). Add more water if they boil dry.

When the beans are cooked, add syrup and vinegar, adjust the seasonings, and serve hot.

SWEDISH MEAT BALLS

3 tablespoons minced onion
2 tablespoons butter
1 pound each beef, veal and pork, ground together
1 tablespoon allspice
1 tablespoon salt (or to taste)
¼ teaspoon ground ginger
¼ teaspoon ground cloves
¼ teaspoon ground nutmeg
½ teaspoon white pepper
1 cup fine dry white bread crumbs
½ cup beef stock
2 eggs
Butter for frying
1 quart beef stock, bouillon or broth
¼ cup flour

Sauté the onion in butter until golden. Combine with all remaining ingredients except the last three, and mix thoroughly by hand. Shape into small balls, and sauté them in a little butter until nicely browned. Remove to a large pot, add the beef stock, and simmer gently for 45 minutes. Refrigerate overnight.

In the morning, remove and reserve any hardened fat from the top, heat the meat balls until the stock melts, and pour off the stock.

Make a roux of ¼ cup reserved fat and ¼ cup flour, add the stock, and cook, stirring, till thickened. Return the meat balls to the sauce, heat through, and serve.

OLD MAN'S HASH

3 large onions, chopped
3 tablespoons butter
12 Swedish anchovy fillets, chopped fine
6 hard-boiled eggs, chopped
1 teaspoon anchovy liquid
¼ cup heavy cream (or more, to taste)

Sauté the onion in butter until transparent. Add the chopped anchovies. Remove from the heat, and add remaining ingredients. Mix well and serve warm.

SAVORY POTATOES

This dish is also known as Janssons Frestelse — *Jansson's Temptation. Whoever Jansson was, he knew his onions, potatoes and anchovies.*

10 potatoes, peeled and sliced
10 Swedish anchovy fillets, cut into small pieces
2 onions, finely chopped
6 tablespoons butter
Salt and white pepper to taste
3 tablespoons flour
1½ cups cream

In a buttered casserole, sprinkle layers of potatoes with anchovies, onions, butter, salt, pepper and flour. End with a layer of potatoes. Pour cream on top; add a little anchovy juice, and salt and pepper. Bake, covered, at 375° for 1 hour. Uncover and continue to bake until brown on top.

HERRING SAVORY

4 salt herring fillets (the whole salt herrings having first been
    soaked for 12 hours in several changes of cold water
    before boning and skinning)
⅓ cup dry bread crumbs
3 tablespoons butter
⅓ cup cream
1 tablespoon chopped chives

Coat the fillets thoroughly with bread crumbs. Butter a small au gratin dish with 1 tablespoon butter, lay in the fillets, dot with the remaining butter, pour over the cream, and bake at 400° for 5 to 10 minutes.

Sprinkle with chopped chives before serving.

MOCK OYSTER PUDDING

5 salt herring roes
⅔ cup bread crumbs
2 cups half and half
6 tablespoons melted butter
5 eggs, beaten
1 teaspoon sugar
A little nutmeg

FOR THE BAKING DISH

¼ cup butter
½ cup fresh bread crumbs

Rinse the roes well and soak for 3 hours. Drain and chop fine. Mix with the bread crumbs, half and half, melted butter, and eggs. Season with sugar and nutmeg. Pour into the buttered and bread-crumbed baking dish. Bake at 350° for 30 to 40 minutes, or until the center is nicely puffed.

PARIS SNACKS

1 pound best-quality lean beef, twice ground
¼ cup bread crumbs, soaked in milk and squeezed out
2 tablespoons capers, chopped fine
2 tablespoons sweet gherkins, chopped fine
¼ cup finely chopped cooked beets
Salt and white pepper to taste
6 to 8 slices white bread
Butter for spreading
Butter for frying

Mix the first six ingredients thoroughly by hand.

Spread the bread slices thickly with butter, and fry on the buttered side till golden brown. Remove from the pan, spread the fried side of the slices thickly with the meat mixture, and fry, meat side first, for 1 to 2 minutes. Turn, brown on the other side, and serve with fried eggs or creamy scrambled eggs.

MAZARIN CAKE

I. SHORTCRUST

1⅔ cups flour
1 teaspoon baking powder
⅓ cup sugar
½ cup butter
1 egg

Sift the flour and baking powder into a bowl, and work in all ingredients in the order given until you have a smooth paste. Set aside.

II. FILLING

2 cups grated almonds
2 cups sugar
1 cup butter
4 eggs
2 teaspoons almond extract

Work the first three ingredients together by hand, and then beat in the eggs with a wooden spoon. Last of all, beat in the almond extract.

III. PREPARATION

4 tablespoons raspberry jam

Divide the shortcrust in two and, using your fingers, press it into two 9-inch tart pans, lining them completely. Spread 2 tablespoons raspberry jam in the bottom of each, and divide the filling evenly between them. Bake at 325° for 1 hour, or until the centers are well puffed. Serve in small wedges. *Makes 2 cakes.*

15

A Chinese Feast

The weather outside is frightful. Bitter cold, driving snow, or bone-chilling damp — whatever it is that February offers, it does nothing to lift the curse that fell on us the day after New Year's, when everybody ran out of future. What the dead of winter needs is a party to look forward to.

Human beings are the only animals whose happiness depends on looking ahead. For a dog, "next Saturday night" is a thought that never even occurs: it will be time enough when it gets here for him to stretch and yawn in front of the fire. But for us, the prospect of a time to come colors all the days before — and colors them a boring gray at that, unless we come up with the brighter idea to entertain.

But what to serve? The old clichés — the stringy Stroganoff, the *coq au vin* nobody has crowed over in years, the curried *quelque chose* that curries no favor at all — make for a Saturday that seems more like a sentence than a future. Something new and different is called for; indeed, so deep are these doldrums, it probably should be something even a bit ambitious. Why not a Chinese feast?

You do not cook Chinese? Never mind. There was once a time you were a stranger even to scrambling eggs. Take heart.

With a few good recipes and a modicum of advice, your entertainment can include even yourself.

Advice first. The basic rule of Chinese menu planning is that you provide for your guests' appetites not by making more of a given dish but by including additional dishes. Each of the recipes that follows will serve two hungry people. Consequently, all four of them, shared around one after another, will do nicely for eight. With six, there can even be seconds.

The other rule is to select dishes that do not all require the same cooking procedure. Among the following recipes, for example, only the shrimp and the chicken dishes are done in the wok at the last minute. The spareribs are simply reheated under the broiler; the pearl balls will be ready in the steamer whenever needed; and the dessert will have been prepared long since.

Accordingly, almost any order of service you choose will be no problem. If you don't mind being away from your guests for one moderately long spell, you might well present the dishes in the order given. That way, you do all the wok cooking in one shot, and are otherwise under no pressure at all. But if you'd rather be away for two shorter times, just serve the shrimp dish second instead of third.

As far as accompaniments are concerned, plain (unsalted) boiled rice should be available for the two more liquid main dishes, and a variety of condiments for the others: some plum sauce and hoisin sauce (available in oriental shops) for the spareribs; and hot mustard, rice vinegar, hot sesame oil, and hot chili paste with garlic (all likewise available) for the pearl balls. Fresh coriander leaves (Chinese parsley) and chopped chives or scallions are good on everything except dessert.

Finally, for the world's simplest way of cooking rice, try this. Wash the rice (any amount) using a pot and a sieve and as many changes of water as you can put up with (fourteen is by no means unreasonable). Then cover the rice with cold water up to the first joint of your middle finger (i.e., to a depth of 1 inch). Put the pot over high heat (lid on) and bring it to a full boil. Remove the lid, let the surface water boil away until it begins to disappear down the "holes" in the rice, then re-cover the pot, turn the heat very low and give it twenty minutes. Fluff with a paddle or fork before serving.

Incidentally, if you happen to have young children watching when you cook rice this way — and if you're not averse to regaling them with fabulous tales — you might give them the following explanation of the "holes."

Raw rice contains invisible Boiling Water Bugs. Normally, they are as inactive as they are unseen; but when the rice water comes to a rolling boil, they frolic and splash about in the pot, much like microscopic otters at play. When the surface water begins to boil away, however, they become first concerned, then frightened. In panic at the prospect of losing their life-giving element, they burrow down into the rice, seeking the water that still remains below — thus making the holes the child so plainly sees.

Of course, if you are asked what happens to the bugs after all the water is absorbed by the rice, you will have to come up with an explanation more fabulous still. My own favorite is that in their anger at the cook who causes their death, they rise and transfigure themselves into White Glue Bugs, thus making the rice sticky in retaliation.

While you're thinking up your own tale to tell, though, here are the recipes.

BARBECUED SPARERIBS

1 rack spareribs
1 teaspoon brown bean sauce
4 cloves garlic, crushed
½ cup water
¼ cup hoisin sauce

¼ cup sugar
¼ cup dark soy sauce
1 tablespoon sherry

Cut the rack of spareribs apart with a cleaver. Then chop the longer ribs in pieces crosswise so that all your pieces are 4 to 6 inches in length.

Warm the remaining ingredients in a saucepan, blend well, and pour over the cut-up ribs. Marinate, refrigerated, 6 hours or more.

Put the ribs, with the marinade, in one layer in a shallow pan, and bake at 350° for an hour or so, turning occasionally. They should be a good color, but not blackened or dry. Warm them under the broiler or over a hibachi before serving.

PEARL BALLS

1 cup sticky rice (or short-grain rice)
1 pound ground beef (or beef and pork)
2 tablespoons minced onion
1 tablespoon minced fresh ginger
1 tablespoon cornstarch
2 egg whites
1 tablespoon sherry
1 teaspoon sesame oil (or more, to taste)
Salt and pepper to taste

Soak the sticky rice (also called glutinous rice, or sweet rice in oriental groceries) in water overnight. Or do the same with ordinary short-grain rice.

Mix the ground meat with all other ingredients, and form the mixture into balls. Roll them in the drained rice until they are completely covered, put them on an oiled plate, and steam for 20 minutes. A covered turkey roaster makes a suitable steamer: simply put some empty tuna-fish cans in the bottom, add an inch or so of water (in the cans, too), rest the plate on the cans, and steam.

SHRIMP WITH KETCHUP SAUCE

2 tablespoons peanut oil
⅛ teaspoon salt
1 clove garlic, crushed
1 slice fresh ginger, crushed
1 pound raw shrimp, shelled and deveined
2 tablespoons sherry
¼ cup hot chicken stock
1 teaspoon light soy sauce
½ cup tomato ketchup
2 tablespoons cornstarch dissolved in cold water

Heat the wok very hot. Add the peanut oil, salt, garlic and ginger, and stir-fry 10 seconds; add the shrimp, and stir-fry for 30 seconds; add the sherry and the stock, and boil for 1 minute; add the light soy sauce and the tomato ketchup, and bring back to the boil. Thicken with the cornstarch mixture, check for salt, and serve.

DICED CHICKEN WITH ALMONDS

2 tablespoons peanut oil (or less)
Salt to taste
1 slice fresh ginger, crushed
1 cup Chinese cabbage, diced
½ cup fresh mushrooms, diced
4 water chestnuts, diced
¼ cup celery, diced
½ cup bamboo shoots, diced
1 cup hot chicken stock
2 tablespoons peanut oil (or less)
2 boned chicken breasts, diced
12 snow peas, diced
2 tablespoons cornstarch dissolved in cold water
½ cup toasted almonds (see below)

Heat the wok hot, add a little peanut oil and salt, then add the ginger, and stir-fry 10 seconds; add the Chinese cabbage, mushrooms, water chestnuts, celery and bamboo shoots, and stir-fry

30 seconds; add the stock, cover, and boil for 2 minutes. Remove all, and set aside.

Heat the wok very hot, add a little more oil and salt, then the chicken, and stir-fry 1 minute.

Return the first mixture to the wok, boil, add the snow peas, thicken with the cornstarch mixture, check the seasoning, and dish up.

Sprinkle the dish with toasted almonds, and serve.

(To make toasted almonds, put a ¼-inch layer of salt in the bottom of a small, heavy frying pan, add whole blanched almonds, and brown them nicely over a medium flame, stirring *constantly* — they burn the minute you turn your back. Garnish the finished presentation with the almonds, and save the salt for Chinese cooking.)

THAI CRYSTAL RICE

1 cup sticky rice
1 can sweetened coconut cream (such as Coco Lopez) —
    or, better yet, make your own coconut cream, as on
    p. 149, and sweeten to taste

Soak the sticky rice for 3 hours (or overnight) in cold water.

Line the bottom of a suitable steamer (e.g., one of the perforated, collapsible, three-legged "flying saucer" type) with damp cheesecloth, put in the soaked rice, and steam it for 1 hour.

Put the steamed rice in a saucepan, add the coconut cream, bring it to a boil, stirring constantly, and set aside, covered.

Serve lukewarm with sliced fresh (or canned) mangoes, pineapples, peaches or strawberries.

There is one more dish so simple, so unusual and so good that I cannot resist tacking on the recipe for it. It's a main course item and it, too, is served with rice.

STEAMED EGGS WITH CHINESE SAUSAGE

2 cups water, boiled for 5 minutes and cooled for 10
4 eggs, lightly beaten
2 tablespoons sherry
1 teaspoon sugar
Salt to taste
3 or 4 scallions (green part too), cut into ¼-inch lengths
3 or 4 Chinese sausages (available in oriental groceries),
    parboiled for 15 minutes, drained, and thinly sliced
Coriander leaves to taste
1 tablespoon soy sauce

Combine the first five ingredients and mix well. (The purpose of boiling the water, by the way, is to drive out the air in it, thus obviating "bubbles" in the finished custard.) Strain the egg mixture into a suitable flat baking dish that will fit into the steamer you intend to use.

Add the next three ingredients to the dish, making sure they are well scattered about.

Put the dish in the steamer and steam for 10 to 15 minutes, or until the center is just set. Drizzle the soy sauce over the top and serve.

16

An Armenian Easter

When it comes to celebrating Easter, household cooks have long known what the church has only lately rediscovered. The celebration cannot be confined to Sunday alone: it pervades even the somber events of the week before.

Prior to the liturgical changes of recent decades, Holy Week tended to be observed as if the resurrection hadn't yet occurred — or, indeed, as if there were some doubt as to whether it would happen at all. The faithful were encouraged to psych themselves into a kind of dramatic make-believe. On Palm Sunday, they were supposed to be elated; at the Last Supper, touched; at the trial, outraged; at the crucifixion, horrified; and at the death, depressed. Only after that — and only as if the resurrection were a total surprise — were they to allow the joy of Easter Day to break through.

No domestic cook, of course, ever gave such a drama houseroom. Easter dinner, like the resurrection itself, had to be in the works long before the event. God might raise the dead, but his miracles stopped short of supplying meals on wheels for Sunday afternoon.

As one cook to another, therefore — and as one whose

Holy Week devotions, more often than not, have included scribbling up shopping lists — let me give you an idea of how the stovetender's liturgy actually works.

Returning home from church on Maundy Thursday night, I realize it is high time, not only for the acts of salvation, but for getting my own act in gear as well. Since all I've done so far is cut some forsythia on Palm Sunday and bring it indoors to force the blooms, I put my mind to settling the menu with my wife. Or, more accurately, to letting her unsettle it until it achieves a tentative, if eclectic, angle of repose: some home-made Eggplant Caponata for the anteprandial, and for dinner, a Grilled Butterflied Leg of Lamb with Egg Lemon Sauce, an Armenian Potato and Cheese Casserole, a Wild Rice Pilaf, and Buttered Asparagus — all in quantities sufficient for six, with the wine and the dessert yet to be determined.

On Friday, therefore, we shop. The legs of lamb are large, so we decide to make an additional presentation from them for variety's sake. I ask the butcher to trim off two pounds of lean meat after butterflying: I'll grind that myself for Sini Kufteh, a casserole of Layered Lamb with Bulgur Wheat. The menu is still eclectic, but the Middle Eastern tilt is becoming pronounced. I add Mashed Buttered Parsnips and choose a good Zinfandel to Americanize things a bit.

On our way home, the question of dessert resolves itself. We make our annual Paschal foray to the candy man and, coming away looking as if we've knocked over a chocolate truck, we decide on something light to round out the meal: Farina Halvah, topped with yogurt, honey and cinnamon. Anyone with an unfilled sweet tooth can make do with chocolate truffles and dipped apricots.

There is church again that night, of course, but when we finally do go to bed, everything is on hand for what I consider the best day of the church year. I'm always happiest when the future for which I hope manages to suffuse the present in which I live. Holy Saturday fills that bill perfectly.

It's the one day I know of that is a hundred percent *tomorrow*. Easter, alas, being an impossible act to follow, often seems to have no future at all. But the totally empty day before it just waits to be filled with acts of hope.

Accordingly, I first knead up a batch of bread and set it to proof. Then I assemble the Potato and Cheese Casserole and the Sini Kufteh and refrigerate them for cooking the next day. Next, I make stock for the sauce from the bones and fat the butcher removed, shape and bake the bread, and put down the lamb for grilling in its marinade.

With this much in hand, it's time to contrive the traditional Easter Even late lunch. I call a friend who I know has to pass a pork store between his place and mine and invite him to celebrate the end of Lent with a 3 P.M. drink. I mention, of course, that he might bring a little ... whatever, if he's so moved, and I am not disappointed. Over the years, this device has provided me with some extraordinary free lunches — not to mention the company it affords the cook at work.

Saturday having run its joyful course, there is only one task left before bed. I put the wild rice in a bowl, pour a kettleful of boiling water over it, and cover it for the night. This process, repeated first thing in the morning and again at noon, "cooks" the rice without cooking, as it were, and results in a greater yield than any other method I know. At the price, I want all the volume I can get.

On Easter morning, the tomorrow that powered all these yesterdays finally becomes only today. Until dessert is served, though, and the cognac poured, the cook is still waist-deep in a present filled with the future. Two more "waters" must go on the rice, church must be attended, the pilaf prepared, the casseroles baked, the vegetables cooked, the sauce made, the halvah created and, somewhere near the end, the lamb itself must find twenty minutes or so in the broiler. (I test the lamb for doneness, by the way, with a metal skewer: I push its point to the center of the thickest part, hold it there for a few seconds, whip it out and touch it to my lips. If it's cold, I keep grilling; if it's nicely warm but not hot, I remove the lamb to a warm place and let it sit to reabsorb its juices; and if it burns my lip, I know I have just ruined fifteen dollars' worth of lamb.)

Admittedly, it takes a fairly coordinated act to get everything on the table at 4 P.M., but by then the celebrants are usually willing to leave the cook a margin for error. (One year I curdled the Egg Lemon Sauce twice and nobody even noticed the delay.) In any case, the recipes follow below. Served on time or not — and on Easter Day or any other — they provide a culinary Alleluia for the keeping of the feast.

POTATO AND CHEESE CASSEROLE

¼ pound (or more) melted butter
6 medium potatoes, peeled and sliced thin
½ teaspoon salt
1 pound Muenster (or mozzarella) cheese, grated coarse
1 teaspoon black caraway seeds (or cumin seeds)
4 large eggs, beaten
¾ cup bread crumbs
¼ cup grated Parmesan cheese
2 tablespoons chopped parsley
1 teaspoon oregano
½ teaspoon pepper

Brush a deep 9-by-12-inch baking dish with some of the melted butter, sprinkle the sliced potatoes with the salt, and layer one third of them in the dish. Brush with some more butter, then add, in succession, one half of the Muenster, another third of the potatoes, the remaining half of the Muenster, and the last installment of the potatoes, brushing on butter and sprinkling in some black caraway seeds at every step.

Pour the eggs over all, spread bread crumbs seasoned with the last four ingredients on top, sprinkle with the remaining butter, and bake at 375° for 45 minutes. *Serves 6.*

CAPONATA
(Eggplant Appetizer)

This tastes better the second or third day, and it is an excellent item for home canning. Simply increase all quantities as needed.

1 large eggplant, cubed
¼ cup olive oil
2 onions, coarsely chopped
2 large stalks celery, coarsely cut crosswise
3 cloves garlic, minced
6 large canned tomatoes, drained and chopped
3 dozen Sicilian olives, stoned, in large pieces
1 3-ounce jar of capers, including vinegar
½ teaspoon thyme or oregano
Salt and pepper to taste

Cube the eggplant (peeled or not), and soak it in salted cold water for 20 minutes. Drain.

In a heavy pot, heat the olive oil and add the onions, celery and garlic. Simmer, covered, till the onions are transparent.

Add the remaining ingredients and simmer till the eggplant is quite tender. Correct the seasoning, adding more vinegar or salt as desired. Serve warm or cool. *Serves 6.*

GRILLED BUTTERFLIED LEG OF LAMB

1 leg of lamb, butterflied (If it's large, trim off 2 pounds of
    lean meat and grind it — 1 pound coarse, 1 pound fine.
    This provides the meat for Sini Kufteh.)

FOR THE MARINADE

¼ cup olive oil
Juice of 1 lemon
3 cloves garlic, minced
½ teaspoon salt
¼ teaspoon thyme

Mix the olive oil, lemon juice, garlic, salt and thyme in a flat baking dish, and place the meat in this marinade for at least 6 hours, turning it over occasionally. (It can be refrigerated overnight, but bring it to room temperature before broiling.)

Preheat the broiler to 500°, place the meat on a rack, and broil as if it were a steak, for 10 minutes on one side and 5 on the other.

Turn the first side back up and check the internal temperature with a metal skewer (see above). For properly pink lamb, continue broiling until the skewer comes out quite warm, but not hot (140°). Remove and let rest in a warm place for 10 minutes. Slice and serve with Egg Lemon Sauce. *Serves 6.*

EGG LEMON SAUCE

4 cups strained, defatted lamb stock (recipe below)
4 egg yolks
¼ cup heavy cream
¼ cup lemon juice
A few grains of cayenne pepper
Salt and white pepper to taste

Boil the lamb stock, uncovered, in an enamel or stainless steel pot until it is reduced to 2 cups.

Place the egg yolks, cream and lemon juice in a deep bowl, and beat thoroughly with a whisk.

While still whisking, pour about half of the hot, reduced stock into the yolk mixture. Pour the contents of the bowl back into the pot with the rest of the stock, and cook over low heat, stirring constantly, until it is thickened. *Do not allow it to boil.* Correct the seasoning and keep warm until needed. *Serves 6.*

LAMB STOCK

Bones, fat and trimmings from 1 leg of lamb
2 cloves garlic, chopped
1 onion, chopped
1 stalk celery, chopped
1 carrot, peeled and chopped
3 sprigs parsley, cut coarse
¼ teaspoon thyme
1 bay leaf
8 black peppercorns
½ teaspoon salt

Place all ingredients in a pot, cover with cold water to a depth of one inch, cover the pot, and bring to a boil slowly. Simmer over very low heat for 3 hours. Strain, cool, and refrigerate overnight. The fat will come off in a single cake in the morning.

SINI KUFTEH
(Layered Lamb with Bulgur Wheat)

FOR THE WHEAT MIXTURE

¾ cup fine bulgur wheat (or 1 cup coarse, processed in an
    electric blender for a few minutes at high speed)
½ cup cold water
1 pound lean lamb, ground fine
1 teaspoon paprika
1 teaspoon salt
¼ teaspoon pepper

Mix all ingredients in a bowl, turn out onto a board, and knead for 10 to 15 minutes, gradually adding another ½ to ¾ cup cold water until the mixture is a smooth, not-too-stiff dough. Refrigerate until needed.

FOR THE FILLING

¼ pound butter
1 pound lamb, coarsely ground
½ green pepper, chopped
5 medium onions, chopped
1 tablespoon paprika
¼ cup minced parsley
1 tablespoon crushed dried basil
½ teaspoon ground allspice
1½ teaspoons salt
½ teaspoon freshly ground black pepper
½ cup chopped walnuts (or pine nuts)

Melt the butter in a skillet, add the meat, and sauté 10 minutes, or until it is lightly browned. Add green pepper and onions, stir, and simmer for 30 minutes, uncovered. Add seasonings and nuts, simmer 5 minutes more, and cool. Refrigerate until needed.

FOR THE DISH

¼ cup melted butter
½ cup hot lamb stock

Brush a deep 9-by-9-inch baking dish with 1 tablespoon butter. Take half of the wheat mixture and spread it evenly in the bottom of the dish. Cover with the filling.

Take the other half of the wheat mixture and, with wet hands, pull off pieces and make thin patties of them. Lay these on top of the filling to cover it as evenly as possible, then smooth the surface with wet hands to blend the patties together.

Brush with the remaining butter and refrigerate until needed.

To cook, preheat oven to 375°, cut the *kufteh* in the dish into squares or diamonds, pour on the hot stock, and bake for ½ hour covered and ½ hour uncovered. *Serves 6.*

WILD RICE PILAF

1 cup raw wild rice
Boiling water
1 teaspoon salt
6 tablespoons butter
2 medium onions, chopped fine

The night before you plan to serve this dish, put the wild rice in a large ceramic or glass bowl and pour over it one teakettleful of boiling water. Cover.

In the morning, drain the rice, return it to the bowl, and pour on another kettleful of boiling water. Cover.

At noon, repeat the process again, this time adding the salt to the water. Cover and let stand for at least two hours. Drain.

To prepare the pilaf: melt the butter in a Dutch oven, simmer the onion until it is transparent, then add the drained rice, mix well, check the seasoning for salt, cover, and keep hot over very low heat until needed. *Serves 6.*

FARINA HALVAH

1 cup sugar
1 cup water
1 cup milk
¼ cup evaporated milk
¼ pound unsalted butter
1 cup farina
½ cup pine nuts (or slivered almonds)
Plain yogurt
Honey
Cinnamon

Combine the first four ingredients in a saucepan, bring to a boil, and cool.

Melt the butter in a large, heavy saucepan, add farina and nuts, and stir constantly over medium heat until the nuts are lightly toasted. Slowly add the cooled liquid ingredients, stirring energetically to break up lumps. When the mixture is well blended, lower the heat and cook, covered, for 15 minutes.

Turn off heat, remove the lid, put a clean, dry dish towel on top of the mixture in the pot, replace the lid, and let it stand for 20 minutes.

Uncover, remove towel, and fluff the *halvah* with a fork to a light, crumbly texture. Break up any lumps that remain. Cover, and keep warm until needed.

When serving, pass dishes of yogurt, honey, and cinnamon, so that guests can season the *halvah* to their tastes. *Serves 6 or 8.*

17

A Swedish Celebration

Now the queen of seasons, bright
With the day of splendor,
With the royal feast of feasts,
Comes its joy to render.

So goes the ancient hymn, giving Easter top billing among the feasts of the church year. In the popular imagination, though, the celebration of Jesus' resurrection runs a distant second to the festival of his birth: one potted lily doth not a Christmas tree make, a bag of jelly beans is no stockingful of gifts, and the Easter Bunny isn't even in the same race as Santa Claus. A good holy day should at least be half full of those honest-to-God materialities that form the very stuff of memories; most Easters, alas, resemble nothing so much as a forgettable rabbit filled with sentimental gas.

Easter does have one advantage, however: its celebration focuses on only two things, Food and Faith. By contrast, when Christmas finally rolls around, you can hardly even see the tree for the woods of commerce and busyness. I think it's high time to capitalize on that advantage — with bumper stickers if necessary: PUT THE DINNER BACK IN EASTER; BE PREPARED FOR THE SUPPER OF THE LAMB.

How do you go about it? By searching your memory for Easter dinners you haven't forgotten and then reviving their traditions. Or by inventing some traditions and then producing Easter dinners you'll never forget. Or by a little of both if, like myself, you're caught somewhere in the middle.

My background as far as family cuisine is concerned is British (from which I remember only roast beef, Yorkshire and plum pudding at Christmas) and Swedish (from which I haven't forgotten a thing — my paternal grandmother was a professional and spectacular cook). But for Easter she invariably cooked a ham; so when I came to create my own version of the feast, I abandoned received tradition and, preferring lamb, resorted to acquired cuisines: French for twenty years, Armenian for ten.

But then it occurred to me: my grandmother made perfectly fabulous lamb dinners at other times. Why couldn't I just take one of those and renew a tradition? The memories were all there, even if they weren't strictly of Easter. There was, for example, her version of the Swedish sit-down cocktail hour: no drinks before dinner; just a first course of *rabiff* (steak tartare) with a pony of cold *akvavit* and a small glass of beer for a chaser (the world's most genteel boilermaker). And then there was a soup: my earliest memory of her table is the sight and smell of steaming veal broth, flecked with parsley, in the very same green-rimmed soup plates I still use. And lamb, naturally: basted, in the Swedish manner, with a cup of coffee — sugar, cream and all. And potatoes *au gratin,* and sweet turnips, and broccoli. And for dessert, Mazarin cake.

There was one memory, however, that did properly belong to Easter. After dinner, on holy days and state occasions, my grandmother smoked a cigar. Or, more accurately, part of a cigar: being not only a tough but a frugal Swede, she cut it in two with a razor, kept the head end for herself, and made my grandfather struggle with the half that came unraveled. She never used tobacco otherwise, and after turning seventy-five went from cigars to cigarettes, but more than any other smoker in the world, she burned herself into my memory.

I like to think of things like that. And at Easter I like to hope that as Jesus himself rose from the dead, so will she, and so will I, and so will all the things themselves. I like to believe that everything we remember, the boilermakers, the broth, the Mazarins, the cigars — the whole gorgeous, earthy world we've held so long in our love — will go home to glory with us when he finally holds us in his love forever.

If you'd like to join me in celebrating that with a brand-new old tradition, here are the recipes. Happy Easter.

RABIFF
(Swedish Steak Tartare — see page 85)

VEAL BROTH

1 large breast of veal, cut up
Water
2 onions, chopped coarse
2 carrots, chopped coarse
2 ribs celery, chopped coarse
A handful of parsley, chopped coarse
1 teaspoon salt
10 white peppercorns
2 whole allspice berries
½ teaspoon marjoram
A few blades of mace

Rinse the veal, put it in a deep pot, add water to a depth of 1 inch, cover, and bring very slowly to a boil. Add all remaining ingredients, and simmer for 2 hours, keeping it just barely at the boil.

Remove the veal, cut off the usable cooked meat, and

reserve it for another use. Return the bones and scraps to the pot and simmer 2 hours more.

Strain, cool quickly, uncovered, and refrigerate overnight. In the morning, remove the cake of fat, bring the broth to the boil again, and reduce it to 1½ or 2 quarts. Garnish with chopped parsley. *Serves 6.*

ROAST LEG OF LAMB

1 leg of lamb, boned, rolled and tied
3 tablespoons butter
3 tablespoons chopped parsley
1 carrot, sliced
1 onion, sliced (optional)
1 teaspoon salt
6 black peppercorns
4 cups hot stock (lamb or chicken) or water
1 cup hot coffee with sugar and cream
Flour

Preheat oven to 450°.

Prick the lamb all over with the point of a sharp knife and rub a mixture of the butter and parsley into the holes. Butter a roasting pan lightly, put in the meat, carrot and onion, and brown them in the oven for 10 to 15 minutes.

Lower the heat to 350°, sprinkle the meat with the salt, and add the peppercorns and 2 cups of stock. Baste every 10 minutes, adding the coffee and the remaining stock gradually. Cook until the roast reaches the internal temperature desired (140° for rare lamb, higher for well done).

Remove the roast to a platter and keep it warm. Strain the pan liquid and skim off the fat. Make a roux (1 tablespoon fat and 1 tablespoon flour for each cup of liquid), cook it briefly, add the liquid to it, whisk till smooth, boil till thickened, and simmer 10 minutes. Pass the sauce with the sliced lamb.

POTATOES AU GRATIN

6 medium-size potatoes, peeled and sliced thin
1 teaspoon salt
¼ teaspoon white pepper
A few gratings of nutmeg
½ small onion, minced fine
1 egg, beaten
½ cup grated fresh Gruyère cheese
1 cup milk
1 cup heavy cream
3 tablespoons butter
¼ cup more grated Gruyère

Mix the first seven ingredients in a bowl. Boil the milk and cream together, add to the bowl, and mix again.

Rub a suitable oven-proof dish with half the butter, arrange the potato mixture in the dish, sprinkle with the remaining cheese, and dot with the rest of the butter.

Bake at 350° until the potatoes are tender (about ¾ hour). If the top is not browned, run the dish briefly under the broiler before serving. *Serves 6.*

SWEDISH TURNIPS

2 large yellow turnips
5 cups water
2 teaspoons salt
¼ cup butter
¼ cup brown sugar
1 teaspoon salt, or to taste
1½ cups thin brown stock (or chicken stock)
¼ teaspoon white pepper

Peel the turnips and cut them into ½-inch cubes. Put in boiling salted water and, when it comes to the boil again, cook 15 minutes. Drain.

Brown the butter lightly in a saucepan, add the turnips,

sprinkle with sugar and salt, and keep on stirring until they are nicely browned. Add the stock and simmer until tender, or about 1 hour. Season with white pepper. *Serves 6.*

BROCCOLI WITH HAZELNUTS

2 bunches broccoli
¼ pound butter
½ cup shelled hazelnuts
Juice of ½ lemon, or to taste
Salt to taste

Remove the florets from the broccoli and rinse them. Reserve the stems for another use.

Bring a pot of water to the boil, salt it to taste, drop the florets in, cook them for a minute or so after the water comes back to the boil, drain, rinse under cold water, and drain again. Set aside.

Melt the butter in a deep pot and sauté the hazelnuts over low heat until the butter is lightly browned and the nuts have turned a few shades darker. Remove from the heat and add the lemon juice.

Before serving, reheat the florets by tossing them in the butter-hazelnut mixture. *Serves 6.*

MAZARIN CAKE

(see page 90)

18

A Springtime Luncheon

Are you sick of the grind? Do you need a change? Would you like to spend Thursday at lunch rather than at work? If your answer to any of those is "Yes, but..." read on. This chapter not only supplies moral and philosophical reasons for getting rid of the "but"; it even gives you recipes to reinforce the "yes."

Of all the temptations of spring, none is more tantalizing than the urge to take a weekday off. Soft sun and balmy breezes, fresh green leaves and bright May flowers all conspire to suggest nine holes of golf, a day at the track, a walk in the woods or even a romp down the primrose path of dalliance.

Too often, though, it comes to nothing. A grim sense of responsibility, plus a failure of imagination about excuses, keeps nearly the whole work force on the job. For every soul brave enough to say "funeral" and mean "ball game," there are a thousand whose consciences scream "you can't" at the merest whisper of "I wish." It may be May, but it might just as well be January the way winter's work ethic keeps them still in chains.

All is not lost, though. There is one rite of spring that can supply even so meek a multitude with the pretext for a personal day off.

In anticipation of summer, volunteer organizations wind down their affairs: the year's work, such as it was, is over, and the only items left on the agendas of committees are public motions of self-congratulation and private maneuvers of political self-preservation. What better way is there for a hard-working group to accomplish both than by calling a noon-day luncheon meeting for eight or twelve officers, movers and shakers? How more lavishly can such chiefs praise each other than by treating themselves to good food and wine after a long year's ingratitude from the Indians? How more effectively can they plot the rolling of logs and the turning out of rascals than by gathering, not in fishbowl restaurants or limelit corri-dors of pseudo-power, but in the intimacy of one of their own homes?

Plainly, there is no better occasion. But there is a difficulty. The phrase "ladies who lunch" springs unfortunately to mind — even to minds of otherwise raised consciousness. Be they male or female, many who consider themselves enlightened take the distinctly unenlightened view that noonday dining in private homes is a social cliché whose day is long since gone. There arises in their minds a stereotypical image com-pounded of two parts blue rinse and five parts mindless chat-ter. Their first response to an invitation may well be no.

They are wrong, of course. Even in the days of depressed consciousness, ladies' lunchtime conversations frequently bore more relation to reality than did, say, the macho banter of the country club men's grill. But there is some logic to their wrongness: if the talk at such luncheons was not full of clichés, the menu was. Chicken tetrazzini ran the memory of a per-fectly acceptable opera singer into the ground; turkey divan did more than any dish to make the human race despair of broccoli; quiches practically obscured the face of the earth; and under and through it all, like a gummy river, flowed a veritable Mississippi of canned mushroom soup.

What is needed therefore to ensure a yes instead of a no

to a luncheon invitation are recipes that are not clichés — dishes that are sufficiently off the beaten buffet to match the freshness of spring. Here they are.

A Chicken Salad, Thai Style, garnished with scallions and coriander leaves. An Asparagus Vinaigrette with cooked garlic cloves. An Apple Salad dressed with olive oil, lemon juice and smoked brisling sardines. An Oyster Casserole with cream and biscuits, after the manner of the Grand Central Oyster Bar Pan Roast. A couple of loaves of home-baked sesame bread. And two desserts: one in honor of the season (Whole Fresh Strawberries with sour cream and brown sugar) and the other in honor of the dental profession (the Original Armenian Cavity Locator, the stunningly sweet bread pastry called Ekmek Khadayif with Khaimak).

Finally, on the grounds that committee proceedings, even celebrative ones, can be dry work, there should be a wine worthy of the occasion. Indeed, if by any chance there are surplus funds over which the group still has control, it should think seriously about as many bottles of a good Gewürztraminer (say, a Joseph Phelps from California) as it will take to wipe out the balance. After all, this time next year maybe *they* will have been the rascals that got turned out.

CHICKEN SALAD, THAI STYLE

FOR THE CHICKEN

2 3-pound chickens, cut into parts
¼-inch-thick slice of ginger, crushed
Water to cover
Salt to taste

Place all the ingredients in a pot, bring to a boil, cook 20 minutes more, remove from the heat, and cool, uncovered.

Separate the meat from the bones, dice it, and reserve. (Return the bones to the pot, and make stock for another use.)

FOR THE DRESSING

3 raw egg yolks
½ teaspoon salt (or to taste)
2 tablespoons lemon juice (or more, to taste)
Pinch of cayenne pepper (or to taste)
2 tablespoons sugar (or to taste)
1 cup peanut oil
Unsweetened pineapple juice

Put the first five ingredients in an electric blender (or in a bowl), beat well and, while still beating, add the peanut oil gradually in a thin stream. At this point, the dressing should have the consistency of mayonnaise. Thin it, as desired, with pineapple juice.

FOR THE GARNISH

Tomato roses (*see page 58*)
Scallion flowers *(see page 57)*
Fresh coriander leaves

Combine the meat and dressing, and dish up. Garnish attractively with tomato roses, scallion flowers and coriander leaves. *Serves 8 or more.*

ASPARAGUS VINAIGRETTE

FOR THE ASPARAGUS

5 to 6 pounds fresh asparagus spears
3 heads of garlic
2 tablespoons olive oil
½ cup water
Salt to taste

Break the asparagus spears in two, saving the lower ends for another use. Tie the upper ends in a bundle with all the tips pointing the same way.

Separate the garlic heads into cloves and peel them.

Put the garlic in the bottom of a pot large enough to hold the bundle of asparagus, standing and covered. Add the olive oil, water, and salt to taste, and boil for 5 minutes. Add the bundle of asparagus spears, cover, and simmer until just tender. Do not overcook. Drain, reserving both the cooking water and the garlic cloves.

FOR THE VINAIGRETTE

½ cup vinegar
2 tablespoons cooking water from asparagus
1 tablespoon Dijon mustard
1 teaspoon anchovy paste
Pinch of sugar
Salt and pepper to taste
1 cup olive oil
Boston lettuce leaves
1 hard-boiled egg, white and yolk chopped separately

Combine the first six ingredients and mix well. Add the olive oil and shake thoroughly. Pour over the asparagus spears and garlic. Allow to marinate several hours at room temperature. Arrange the asparagus and garlic on lettuce leaves and, before serving, reshake the dressing, pour it over, and garnish with chopped egg. (Cooked garlic, by the way, is mild and perfectly edible.) *Serves 8 or more.*

APPLE SALAD

Juice of ½ lemon
4 to 6 medium-sweet firm apples (Red Delicious, for example)
2 to 3 large heads of romaine lettuce, broken up
6 tablespoons lemon juice (or to taste)
Pinch of sugar (or to taste)
Salt and pepper to taste
½ cup olive oil
1 or 2 cans brisling sardines

Squeeze the lemon juice into a large salad bowl, core and peel the apples, cut them into thin slices, put them in the bowl, and toss gently to coat with lemon juice. Add the lettuce to the bowl.

Mix the next three ingredients thoroughly, add the olive oil, and mix again.

Just before serving, add the sardines to the salad bowl, mix the dressing again, pour it over the salad, and toss everything gently. *Serves 8 or more.*

OYSTER CASSEROLE

½ cup butter
1 quart shucked oysters
Juice of ½ lemon
1 tablespoon paprika
¼ teaspoon celery seed
3 tablespoons chili sauce
3 cups prepared biscuit mix
1 cup milk
2 cups heavy cream
1 cup milk
1 tablespoon Worcestershire sauce
Salt and white pepper to taste

Coat the inside of a large, flat casserole with 2 tablespoons of butter. Spread the oysters in the bottom and sprinkle them with the lemon juice, 2 teaspoons of paprika and the celery seed. Dot the remaining butter and the chili sauce over all.

Stir the biscuit mix and the first cup of milk together gently to form a soft dough and drop it by spoonfuls on top of the oysters. Spread it out fairly evenly, using fingertips dipped in milk. Sprinkle 1 teaspoon paprika over the top.

Combine the remaining ingredients, pour over the biscuit mixture (breaking the fall with a spoon), and bake at 350° for 40 minutes, or until nicely browned on top. The liquid will run under the biscuit mixture as it rises. To serve, simply cut straight down with a spoon, taking up some oysters, some sauce and some biscuit for each helping. *Serves 8 or more.*

STRAWBERRIES

2 quarts fresh strawberries, washed but not hulled
2 cups sour cream
2 cups brown sugar

Set out these ingredients in three separate bowls, and let guests arrange their own desserts, putting some strawberries, some sour cream and some brown sugar on a plate. The berries are simply dipped into the other ingredients and eaten by hand. *Serves 8 or more.*

BREAD PASTRY
(Ekmek Khadayif)

2 cups sugar
1½ cups water
1 tablespoon lemon juice
2 tablespoons honey
Butter for dish
1 box zwieback
1 cup heavy cream
Cinnamon

Boil the sugar and water together for 5 minutes, remove from the heat, and stir in the lemon juice and honey.

Line the bottom of a buttered 9-by-12-inch baking dish with a single layer of zwieback that have been dipped in cream, and sprinkle them with a little cinnamon.

Pour the hot syrup over the zwieback and bake at 375° for 45 minutes. Cool.

Serve, in smallish portions, with a spoonful of Clotted Cream. *Serves 8 or more.*

CLOTTED CREAM
(Khaimak)

2 cups heavy cream
2 tablespoons sugar
Pinch of salt

Put the cream into a wide saucepan and boil it down by half, stirring constantly. At the end, stir in the sugar and salt, pour into a shallow container, and refrigerate till needed.

19

A Spanish Picnic

It is early summer. August's long-awaited vacation time still seems ages away, but by the same token, its torpor-producing heat and mildew-generating humidity have not yet arrived. Instead, these cool, end-of-June days practically insist on getting the picnic season under way immediately. But, alas, there is a difficulty: alfresco dining has a bad name among us. Tenth-rate hot dogs, carbonized chicken parts and beef à la charcoal lighter are principally what come to mind when we hear the words "outdoor food."

All is not lost, though. What follow here are some rules for restoring not only good food but even a measure of civility to the institution of the picnic lunch. They fall into three categories: personnel, location and food.

Personnel. A picnic lunch for human beings should involve not less than one adult couple nor more than two. The reason for this restriction is twofold. First, since summer weather is notoriously unpredictable, no prudent person will try to arrange a picnic earlier than the night before. Second, no one who is compos mentis would even think of including children in a luncheon meant to be enjoyed by adults. Minor offspring in-

capable of fending for themselves should be handed a can of
Spaghetti-O's and fobbed off on the neighbors.

Location. Unless you actually enjoy spending hours behind
the wheel, the best place for a picnic lunch is always the shortest
haul from home. Begin by seriously considering your own back
yard and reject that, if you must, only in favor of the nearest
green space you can legally land on. Part of the pleasure of
picnicking is the enjoyment of having less than usual to do.
People who commit themselves to logistical feats worthy of the
Normandy invasion have a questionable sense of how to spend
a day off.

Food. The sovereign rule here is one that modern America
has practically lost sight of: the enjoyment of food increases
with one's distance from the cooking. Outdoor eating is tolerable
only if you can manage to do it someplace away from the smoke,
the flies and the human traffic jams that usually attend it — and
it is splendid only when those circumstances are not present at
all. In other words, if you want to have a decent picnic, prepare
every last scrap of it in the kitchen, leaving yourself no reason
whatsoever to sit next to hot charcoal. Since that move away
from the fire was probably the very second step toward civiliza-
tion the caveman took, it's a shame to go back on it at this late
date.

Therefore, putting all those rules into practice, behold the
civilized picnic lunch for four. Each person's meal is neatly
encased in a bakery box; inside that, items that can't conve-
niently be wrapped are enclosed in delicatessen containers. The
menu — no more than a few hours' work on the evening before
and the morning of the day itself — is of the Spanish persuasion:
gazpacho, a meat sandwich, a chickpea salad and a flan for
dessert. And the wine? Well, make it wines, to ensure fes-
tivity: how about a Harvey's Amontillado with the soup and
Marques de Caceres *rioja* with the rest? But beware. Civili-
zation is a fragile thing. You could get everything else right

and destroy the whole picnic with Styrofoam cups. It's taken us 5,000 years to get this far. Let's have honest-to-goodness stemware only, please — just to keep us reminded of our responsibilities.

GAZPACHO
(Andalusian Salad Soup)

Prepare this the night before.

1 clove garlic, crushed
2 thick slices stale Italian bread, broken up
½ cup water
¼ cup olive oil
1 large can tomatoes and juice, seeds removed
1 can tomato paste
¼ cup chopped onion
¼ cup chopped pimiento
¼ cup sherry vinegar, or to taste (¼ cup cider vinegar plus
    2 teaspoons dry sherry will do for a substitute)
2 to 3 cups cold water
Salt to taste
Chopped hard-boiled egg
Seeded and chopped cucumber
Chopped green pepper
Chopped onion
4 green-pepper halves

Mix garlic, bread, water and olive oil in a bowl, and let stand several hours.

Put contents of bowl into an electric blender (or a food processor), add tomatoes, paste, onion and pimiento, and purée. (It may be necessary to do this in two batches.) Chill thoroughly.

When ready to pack the lunch, add the vinegar and enough cold water to bring the soup to the desired consistency. Add salt to taste, and pour into a suitable insulated container. Place chopped egg, cucumber, pepper, and onion separately into pepper halves, wrap in plastic wrap, and serve as garnishes for each person to add as desired.

MEAT SANDWICHES

6 tablespoons olive oil
2 tablespoons vinegar
1 teaspoon minced onion
1 tablespoon minced fresh coriander leaves
Salt and pepper to taste
1 pound cold roast meat (pork, beef or lamb), preferably
    not overcooked, sliced very thin
8 slices from the center of a large, round loaf of homemade
    bread or Italian bread
Butter
⅔ cup homemade mayonnaise made with olive oil (or a
    commercial, nonsweet mayonnaise into which several
    tablespoons of olive oil have been beaten)
Boston lettuce
Salt and pepper
Coriander leaves for garnishing

Prepare a marinade from the first five ingredients. Dip the slices of meat in the marinade, put them in a bowl, pour any remaining marinade over, and let them stand for 1 hour.

Take four slices of bread and spread each liberally with butter and mayonnaise (using up about ⅓ of the mayonnaise altogether). Add a layer of lettuce leaves to each slice, salt and pepper to taste, put ¼ pound sliced meat (drained briefly of marinade) on each, spread on more mayonnaise (using another ⅓ cup), and add another layer of lettuce leaves. Spread butter and remaining mayonnaise on the other four slices of bread, complete the sandwiches, cut them into fours (three straight cuts forming an *N* make four nice pieces), garnish with coriander leaves, wrap well, and refrigerate till needed.

GARBANZOS SALTEADOS
(Chickpea Salad)

This too should be prepared the night before.

3 tablespoons olive oil
1 medium onion, minced
1 or 2 cloves garlic, minced
1 20-ounce can chickpeas, drained
1 large fresh tomato (or several canned), chopped
¼ cup minced parsley
¼ cup chopped ham or chorizo (Spanish sausage)
Salt to taste

FOR THE GARNISH

Tomato wedges
Green pepper rings
Carrot flowers *(see page 61)*

Simmer onions and garlic in olive oil until transparent but not brown. Add chickpeas, tomato, parsley, ham and salt as desired. Cook briefly, cool to room temperature, put into four half-pint (or pint) delicatessen containers, garnish attractively, and cover securely.

FLAN
(Caramel Cup Custard)

Once again, prepare this the night before.

½ cup sugar
6 custard cups (glass or ceramic)
2 cups milk
½ cup cream
⅓ cup sugar
⅓ cup honey
Pinch of salt
2 whole eggs plus 3 yolks
½ teaspoon vanilla extract
3 tablespoons good Scotch whisky (or Drambuie or
    Spanish brandy)

Preheat oven to 300° or 325°.

Put ½ cup sugar in a dry, heavy saucepan and let it melt over low to moderate heat. Do not stir until it is nearly all melted, but do not let it get any darker than necessary. When it is completely liquid, pour some of this caramelized sugar into each of the custard cups. Do this one cup at a time, rotating the cup to allow the caramel to coat the bottom and lower sides completely.

Put the milk, cream, sugar, honey and salt in a saucepan, and scald slowly over low heat to dissolve the sweeteners — and to drive the air out of the milk, thus preventing bubbles in the finished custard. Cool slightly.

Beat the eggs lightly in a bowl, add the milk mixture, vanilla and liquor, mix well, and strain into the custard cups.

Stand the cups in a baking pan, add hot water to a depth of 1 inch, and bake at 300° or 325° for 20 to 30 minutes, or until the centers have just set. Remove from the oven, cool, and refrigerate thoroughly.

To pack for the picnic, run a thin knife around the inside of the cup to free the sides of the custard, invert a half-pint delicatessen container over the cup, and then invert both so that the custard and the caramel syrup will be deposited in the container. Cover and chill till needed.

20

A Surfeit of Eggplants

Let us sing the praises of seasonal glut. Summer, at last, has come all the way in: eggplants — glossy, wine-dark and firm — are everywhere. Away then with listless refrains: *I got the crudités blues; Myra's prob'ly makin' ratatouille again.* The song for this season is *Invention!*

And the singers? Who else but those who fiddle with eggplants in both garden and kitchen? No matter how they come by these spectacular members of the nightshade family — whether from their own back yards, or from friends', or from farm stands they simply cannot bear to pass — it is precisely too much of such a good thing that inspires them to shelve the old set pieces and improvise.

When the full history of the human race is finally recited in heaven, there will, I think, be a small eternity devoted to midsummer afternoons. For it is in just such times of desperate leisure — when creative souls have no alternative but to take what is at hand and imagine hitherto unimagined uses for it — that the arts and sciences have made their gigantic steps forward.

Backward, too, no doubt. There will probably be a parallel recitation in hell of the misuse of those long afternoons: grim ballads recounting the invention of the MX missile and the ceramic cooktop; tuneless dirges celebrating serial music, TV dinners and instant rice.

But in heaven only the successes will be sung: triumphal lays, for example, to the genius who, after working his way through five burlap bagsful of bluefish in the summer of '71, perfected Bluefish Provençale; an oratorio for the mere novice of a cook who, half buried under fresh asparagus the next spring, put the world forever in her debt with Asparagus Lemon Cream Sauce for pasta. And, if one may dare to hope, at least eight bars for the writer and his wife who, in the summer of '81, invented Indo-Armenian Eggplant Halvah with Clotted Cream and Pistachios.

But such eschatological thoughts get us ahead of the story. My 1981 fit of eggplantomania began, as I recall, on a particularly long Saturday afternoon late in June. I had just wandered in from the garden, and I observed to my wife that the eggplants were coming along splendidly. We would have firstfruits come August. "Well," she replied, "I certainly hope you're going to do something different with them this year. One more of those quarter-acre panfuls of Imam Bayeldi and *you'll* be the priest who faints. Not from delight, either. I'll call my lawyer."

Sentences like that, as Dr. Johnson remarked, focus the mind wonderfully. So she wanted different dishes, did she? Well, she would have them. And not just in due season. I went out and bought a dozen eggplants then and there.

Returning, I put them on the table in imitation of midsummer's bounty and announced that this was one project I refused to tackle alone. She would think with me, or else the whole lot could go to squishy ruin. To my surprise, she had been thinking already. "How about eggplants for dessert?" she asked brightly. "They smell like bananas when you cut them up. Why can't you adapt a banana recipe and make something completely new?"

One of the disadvantages of knowing a fair amount about a subject is the ease with which you come to assume you know everything about it. "An eggplant dessert?" I said patronizingly. "Come now. That's one of the few follies the human race seems to have avoided. Why should we break a five-thousand-year winning streak?"

She made an unkind remark about chefs who talked through their *toques blanches,* but added that if I'd just keep the sweet eggplant dish in mind, she'd favor me with some of her other thoughts. Hoping vainly that the idea would go away, I mumbled agreement.

Sensing irresolution, she took the offensive. "First of all, I will not nosh on another *babaghanoosh* until you've made lots of other things with eggplant. If you have to repeat yourself, how about two things you haven't made in years? The eggplant and meat casserole and the fried eggplant salad?"

I refrained from pointing out that I had made both as recently as last October. A customer with a short memory is easier to please than one who is always right. "Fair enough," I said. "What else?"

"That's better," she said. "Now. How about deep-fried eggplant? You never make that anymore, either. Think of new coatings, though."

She meant, of course, something other than the usual breading of flour, egg and crumbs. Several possibilities suggested themselves: beer batter; a cornstarch, soy sauce and sherry mixture; the oil, flour, baking powder and water batter for Chinese puffed shrimp; and an Indian preparation with a soy flour base. I mentioned these to her.

"That would be nice," she said. "Let's have it tonight."

Needless to say, by "it" she meant all of them — "so we can compare," as she put it. "It'll be fun."

"Frying five different kinds of fritters for one dinner is not exactly my idea of fun," I told her. "But now that I think of it, that Indian batter gives me an idea. Remember the okra curry I made once? Well, eggplant thickens up a bit like okra. Why couldn't I just make eggplant curry instead?"

"Good," she said. "You're finally getting into the mood. That'll be a nice contrast to the fritters."

"You mean tonight?"

"Of course," she said. "And what's more, I think I've solved the dessert problem. Remember the Indian Banana Halvah?"

"You don't mean that pasty rosewater stuff, do you? You hated it."

"So leave out the rosewater and put in lemon or something. I bet you it'll be terrific."

To give a long afternoon short shrift, so it was. I wish I could claim I went gladly to the invention of Eggplant Halvah, but in fact I had to be dragged kicking and screaming through the whole creative process. When the eggplant mixture itself was perfected, she said it still needed something. Pistachios, she decided. After I went out for pistachios (and a small loan on the way from the bank's money machine) she said it looked naked without clotted cream on top. Back to the store again for heavy cream . . .

But perhaps that will do. The recipes follow below. They are all good and I commend them to you the next time you find yourself waist-deep in eggplants. The dessert, however, is not just good: it may be the only thing you serve this year that absolutely nobody has ever tasted.

EGGPLANT AND MEAT CASSEROLE

1 large eggplant, about 2 pounds
Salt
2½ pounds ground lamb (or beef)
1 medium-size onion
2 teaspoons paprika
½ teaspoon ground allspice
½ teaspoon pepper
2 teaspoons salt
½ cup chopped parsley
2 medium-size potatoes

2 medium-size zucchini
2 large, firm tomatoes
1 cup tomato sauce *(see page 48)*
½ cup water

Cut the stem off the eggplant, slice it in half lengthwise and then into ½-inch slices crosswise, sprinkle all the pieces with salt, and let them stand in a bowl while you make the meat mixture.

Mix the meat thoroughly with the next six ingredients.

Peel the potatoes and cut them into ¼-inch slices. Remove the stems from the zucchini and slice likewise. Do the same with the tomatoes.

Butter a 9-by-14-inch baking dish. Rinse the eggplant slices, and pat dry.

Take an eggplant slice, stand it vertically at one end of the dish, pull off a little of the meat mixture (about the size of a walnut), and press it flat against the eggplant. Press a zucchini slice against that, then more meat against the zucchini, then a potato slice against that, more meat against the potato, a tomato slice against that, more meat against the tomato, then an eggplant slice again, and so on — making two or three rows of such "sandwiches" until the dish is filled.

Mix the tomato sauce and water, pour over the meat and vegetables, cover with aluminum foil, and bake at 400° for 30 minutes. Uncover and bake for about 30 minutes more (or until the vegetables are tender); but do not let it dry out. *Serves 6.*

FRIED EGGPLANT SALAD

1 medium-size eggplant
Salt
1 medium-size onion
1 clove garlic
½ teaspoon salt
¾ cup olive oil
Juice of 1 lemon

Peel the eggplant, cut it lengthwise into ½-inch slices, then cut the slices in half crosswise. Sprinkle the pieces with salt and let them stand in a bowl for 30 minutes.

Slice the onion very thin crosswise, mince the garlic, and mix both together with ½ teaspoon salt.

Rinse the eggplant slices and pat dry. Heat the oil in a skillet and fry the slices until golden brown.

Put a layer of fried slices in the bottom of a deep dish, spread some of the onion mixture over it, sprinkle with lemon juice, and then continue layering until all the ingredients are used. Refrigerate several hours before serving. *Serves 4.*

FIVE COATINGS FOR EGGPLANT FRITTERS

To use any of these, it is convenient to peel the eggplant at the last minute, cut it in half lengthwise and into ¼-inch slices crosswise, and then proceed directly to the coating and frying. If you wish, you may salt and rinse the slices, as above, but be sure to dry them as much as possible before coating.

I

1 egg
1 tablespoon water
½ cup flour
1 teaspoon salt
¼ teaspoon pepper
1 cup fine bread crumbs

Put the egg in a large bowl, add the water, and beat well.

Mix the flour, salt and pepper in a large paper bag, add all the eggplant slices at once, and shake well.

Empty the bag onto a counter top and then transfer the slices to the bowl of beaten egg, leaving behind as much loose flour as possible. Turn the slices over in the egg until uniformly coated.

Put the bread crumbs in the paper bag, put in all the eggplant slices again, and shake well. If necessary, add more bread crumbs.

Empty the bag once again, spread the slices out on a rack to let the coating set for 15 minutes or more, and fry in deep, hot oil (375°). Drain on paper and serve.

II

1½ cups flour
1 teaspoon salt
¼ teaspoon pepper
1 tablespoon vegetable oil
2 eggs, well beaten
¾ cup flat beer (approximately)

Mix the first five ingredients together, then stir in beer until the batter is fluid but still a bit elastic. Let rest for several hours in the refrigerator. When ready, dip eggplant slices in the batter and deep-fry (375°).

III

2 tablespoons soy sauce
2 tablespoons saké or dry sherry
2 tablespoons peanut oil
½ teaspoon sugar
¼ teaspoon pepper
Cornstarch

Put the eggplant slices in a large bowl. Add everything but the cornstarch and mix well. Sprinkle on cornstarch and continue mixing until a thin but fairly viscous coating is achieved. Deep-fry (375°).

IV

This one puffs up handsomely; fry fewer slices at one time.

1½ cups flour
1 tablespoon baking powder
½ teaspoon salt
½ cup peanut oil
Cold water

Mix the first four ingredients in a bowl until well blended into a dough. Gradually stir in cold water (1 cup, more or less) until a batter is formed. It should have the consistency of half-whipped cream. Dip the eggplant slices in it and deep-fry (375°).

V

¼ cup soy flour
1 teaspoon salt
¼ teaspoon ground turmeric
½ teaspoon ground cardamom (or 1 teaspoon ground
    coriander seed)
Cold water

Mix the first four ingredients in a bowl and stir in enough water to make a batter the consistency of half-whipped cream. Dip the eggplant slices in it and deep-fry (375°).

EGGPLANT CURRY

1 medium-size eggplant
Salt
2 large onions, chopped coarse
¼ cup vegetable oil
1 tablespoon curry powder
1 teaspoon lemon juice
3 tomatoes, peeled and chopped coarse, with juice
Salt

Peel the eggplant, cut it into 1-inch cubes, salt it, and let it stand in a bowl.

Fry the onions in the oil until golden brown in a pot or deep skillet large enough for the finished dish.

Lower the heat, add the curry, and stir for a few minutes. Rinse the eggplant, drain, and add to the pot. Add lemon juice, and simmer, stirring frequently, for 5 minutes.

Add the tomatoes, and salt if necessary. Simmer 10 minutes more, stirring frequently. Add a little water if it becomes too dry. Serve with rice. *Serves 4.*

EGGPLANT HALVAH

Juice of 1½ lemons, or to taste
1 cup sugar
1½ cups water
1 large eggplant, about 2 pounds
¼ pound salted butter
1 teaspoon ground (preferably freshly pounded) cardamom
½ cup pistachios
1 recipe clotted cream *(Khaimak: see page 122)*

Put the lemon juice in a large bowl.

Boil the sugar with 1 cup of water and set aside.

Peel the eggplant, cut it into dice, and toss the pieces in the bowl with the lemon juice.

Melt the butter in a deep saucepan, empty the bowl into the saucepan, add ½ cup water, and cook over medium heat, covered, stirring frequently, until the eggplant is soft (about 20 minutes). Add a little more water if it threatens to brown.

Mash the eggplant as thoroughly as possible in the pot, add the sugar syrup, and cook, uncovered, stirring constantly, until it has the consistency of very thick oatmeal. Remove from the heat, and stir in the cardamom.

Sprinkle the pistachios over the bottom of a deep 9-by-9-inch baking dish, add the eggplant and, when cool, top with clotted cream. Refrigerate thoroughly (at least six hours), divide into squares, and serve. *Serves 9.*

21

A Japanese Barbecue

There can be little argument that when Americans entertain they display an almost religious devotion to barbecuing. In any weather except drifting snow or pouring rain, there arises from country lawns, suburban yards and city rooftops the smoke of fat calves and full-fed beasts, the sweet savor that improves everyone's outlook on life — even, the Bible assures us (Genesis 8:21), that of the LORD himself.

But alas, as with so many religions, its devotees often fail to do justice to their faith. Some — let us call them the Low Church, or just-give-me-plain-burnt-meat practitioners — hardly seem to have any practices at all. Charcoal fires are lit, of course, but with a petroleum starter whose smell permeates everything. Great slabs of indifferent beef are cooked (if that is the word for meat that is either nine-tenths raw or vulcanized to the consistency of a shoe heel). They are sliced up (if hacking can be dignified with such a description), and they are passed around on paper plates that invariably collapse, depositing the dinner on the driveway. Worse yet, hamburger patties hoary with frost are incinerated by teenagers, while hot dogs are poked unceremoniously into the fire by five-year-olds.

On the other hand, there are the High Church, or leave-religion-to-the-clergy-alone believers. You know their exclusively male priesthood well. The Reverend Host is about to pontificate over the charcoal: let mere laypersons withdraw to a respectful distance while he brushes and dabs, turns and tests — generally taking forever to produce even a morsel, and all the while boring everybody stiff with sermons on the one true sauce.

It was on a trip to Japan that a way out of this barbecuing either/or was opened up. We were a party of four being entertained alfresco in a small city outside Tokyo. What greeted us after a walk through a park was one of the few sensible cookouts we had ever attended.

Braziers had been lit, and the foods to be cooked were tastefully laid out on a table. There were small whole fish, large shrimp, individual lamb, beef and pork cutlets, fresh mushrooms, onions and green peppers, potatoes in foil and rice shaped into patties. Where necessary, skewers had been used to make items manageable. On the side were sauces for brushing and dipping. Best of all, each of us was not only allowed, but expected to cook.

Yakimono (literally, "grilled things") is one of the oldest and most extensive categories of Japanese cuisine. Perhaps by very reason of its long history, it seems mercifully free from both the under- and the over-enthusiasms with which we approach grilling here. On the one hand, it is anything but carelessly thrown together: the cook, well before guests arrive, has done what can amount to an honest half day's work of boning, slicing, dicing and skewering — not to mention preparing marinades, toppings and dips. But on the other, more merciful hand, he or she does not have to obtrude dogmatically on the subsequent proceedings. With a minimum of advice, guests choose and cook their food by their own lights.

Accordingly, here is some general advice, plus a number of specific suggestions that will enable you to lift the twin curses of too little or too much fuss from your outdoor cooking.

First, the generalities.

On charcoal. Use the best you can afford (preferably not impregnated with anything). And don't light it with boom juice. Instead, use paper to light a fire of kindling wood and then put the charcoal on top of that. Above all, get the charcoal going well ahead of time so you have glowing, and not half-lit coals to cook over.

Grills. Hibachis are nice for two, but for a crowd, a big, flat, round job will give you a much better performance. In particular, it will enable you (by piling the hot coals higher on one side of the grill than on the other) to maintain two temperatures: one very hot, for things like shrimp and small fish that should be well done on the outside before the middle is barely cooked; the other moderate, for things like steaks and vegetables that may need more time.

Ingredients. A "mixed" grill is best: poultry, meat, seafood, vegetables. The suggestions that follow will provide you with ideas for all four, as well as for marinades and toppings.

Skewers. Have plenty of both long (12-inch) and short (6-inch) bamboo skewers, as well as toothpicks, on hand before you begin preparations. The oriental grocery you visit to buy other ingredients can supply you.

Now for the specifics. (Ingredients marked with an asterisk below are available in oriental groceries.)

Chicken. The best parts for barbecuing are the wings and the leg-thigh pieces (breast meat dries out too easily). Leg pieces can, of course, be left unboned and cooked either whole or cut in two; but if you have the patience to skin and bone them and then cut the meat into 1-inch dice to be threaded on skewers, your guests will love you for it.

For example, you can set out before them a whole tray of chicken delights ready for grilling: leg-thigh squares on some skewers; halved livers on others; and, on yet others, parboiled hearts and gizzard pieces, leg meat alternated with scallion pieces, and 1-inch-wide strips of chicken skin pleated up accordion-fashion.

All of these can be grilled over hot charcoal as is and brushed with a marinade near the end; or they can be marinated briefly (30 minutes is fine) and then cooked. (Just remember: Japanese marinades tend to be sweet and therefore blacken easily; heavy applications should be made only near the end of the cooking.)

Marinades. Use commercially bottled teriyaki sauce; or make your own sauces as follows.

TERIYAKI SAUCE

1 cup saké
1 cup *mirin*° (sweet cooking saké)
1 cup Japanese soy sauce
1 tablespoon sugar (or more to taste)

Boil to dissolve sugar. Cool and use.

QUICK YAKITORI SAUCE

1 cup saké
¾ cup Japanese soy sauce
3 tablespoons *mirin*°
2 tablespoons sugar (or more to taste)

Boil to dissolve sugar. Cool and use.

Needless to say, whole, boned chicken thighs (skin-on, and skewered flat), as well as small steaks, lamb chops and pork cutlets can be brushed with these marinades toward the end of cooking.

Seafood. The business of skewering has been developed to a fine art by the Japanese, and the names of the various techniques practically explain themselves. For the record, they are: flat-skewering, fan-skewering, side-skewering, one- and two-sided tucking for fish fillets and finally, wave-skewering for whole fish.

Small whole fish, e.g., whitebait, shiners. If guests have the nerve for them, they will find these ungutted, unbeheaded little fellows delicious — not unlike fried clams in taste. Fan-skewer three or four fish on three skewers.

Larger whole fish (heads on, but gutted and scaled), e.g., snappers (baby bluefish). Wave-skewer these so that the skewers always enter and exit the fish on the same side (thus leaving the other side unblemished).

Shrimp. Fan- or side-skewer four or five shrimp on three skewers (having first made a longitudinal cut all along the underside of each shrimp to inhibit curling).

Fillets of fish. Use fillets with the skin on. Cut them into 1-inch-wide strips and skewer, skin side out, tucking in and up either one or both ends depending on length.

Clams. Wash hard clams, coat them with lots of coarse salt while still damp, and place them level on the grill over hot charcoal. Lay a loose "tent" of aluminum foil over them, and cook 2 to 3 minutes.

For guests who may prefer to grill their selections without marinades, however, set out some sauces for dipping. (Don't forget, though, a squeezing of juice from a lemon wedge is hard to beat — as is plain Japanese soy sauce, especially on a foil-wrapped potato with butter.)

LEMON SOY

Mix lemon juice into Japanese soy sauce to taste.

MUSTARD SOY

Mix dry mustard powder (preferably Japanese*) into a paste with water, let it stand briefly to develop flavor, and dissolve it to taste in soy sauce.

GINGER SOY

Grate 1 or 2 tablespoons fresh ginger.* on the finest grater you have. Put the gratings into a tea strainer, and press the juice into a cup. Add soy sauce to taste. Discard pulp.

WASABI

Mix dry *wasabi* horseradish powder* with water into a paste, let it stand to develop flavor, and thin it to a manageable consistency with more water. (Be sure, though, to warn guests that this is dynamite: it blasts straight at the base of the skull.)

Finally, for something different to put on skewered vegetables (particularly eggplant, and tofu, or bean curd) try these *miso** toppings. *Miso* is a fermented bean paste that comes in many colors and flavors from light tan ("white" *miso*) to almost black. Most varieties are quite salty.

To use these toppings, simply grill skewered eggplant slices, large whole mushrooms, tofu pieces (two small skewers to a piece, please) until done; then spread the *miso* topping on one side only and return to the grill briefly (1 or 2 minutes) to heat the topping. The result is called eggplant, or tofu, or whatever, *dengaku.*

DENGAKU RED MISO TOPPING

½ cup red *miso**
3 tablespoons white *miso**
2 egg yolks
2 tablespoons saké
2 tablespoons *mirin**
2 tablespoons sugar
7 tablespoons *dashi,** or water (*see note*)

Put both kinds of *miso* in the top of a double boiler; blend in egg yolks, saké, *mirin* and sugar. Place over simmering water, and gradually stir in *dashi* or water. Cook, stirring, until thickened. Season to taste with one of the following: grated lemon rind, fresh ginger juice, ground toasted sesame seeds. Cool. Keeps well refrigerated.

Note. Dashi, the basic soup stock of Japanese cooking, is made from kelp and dried bonito shavings. Powdered instant *dashi,* however, is available in oriental groceries.

22

A Thai Sampler

Thai restaurants are in fashion. The cuisine's fragrant, incendiary dishes — served invariably on glass-topped tables with the cloths underneath the glass — are everywhere in major cities, and they've begun to invade the suburbs as well. Sadly though, Thai cooking in the home is still rare. To remedy that defect, here is the encouraging story of one cook's five-year romance with Thai food: I actually began cooking it before the fad began.

Admittedly, the claim to being ahead of one's time is usually a form of long-range self-praise designed to explain the short-term absence of fame and fortune from an allegedly brilliant career. In my own case, however, the phrase has a happier, if narrower meaning: I have a peculiar knack for discovering trends, not decades but practically minutes ahead of everyone else. Let me give you a random sampling of my head starts.

I established a wine cellar in 1952, just before America discovered wine — and when Corton-Charlemagne, believe it or not, went for $55 a case. I bought my first wok in the mid-fifties, hardly four days prior to the invention of the first "gourmet" cookware shop. I grew my beard in '64, six weeks, as I recall, before facial hair sprouted everywhere; and I took up running in '67, just ahead of the detestable army of joggers who turned it into a statistical exercise less fun than a treasurer's report. By a matter of seconds almost, I seem always to have been the old-timer who was already there when everyone else arrived.

It was by exactly that streak of luck that my discovery of Thai cooking took place in the summer of '77. From June to August we lived in my old neighborhood in Queens, trying to get fortune, if not fame, from the sale of the family house. The Scotch-Irish Jackson Heights of my childhood had long since vanished, of course, having been overlaid by a profusion of South American identities. We looked forward to an orgy of Peruvian, Argentinian, Ecuadorean — and above all, China-Latina eating.

On our first night out we scouted the territory, reading the menus sensibly posted in the front window of every restaurant. A small Thai establishment was the first we came to, and even though we shopped a dozen more, something kept drawing me back to it. "There's plenty of time for the others," I said craftily; "tonight let's eat Thai. If the neighborhood's going oriental, why not be the first on the bandwagon?"

To make a delicious story short, we never ate anywhere else. Three nights a week, twelve weeks in a row, we tasted our way through the entire menu. And on the off nights, with the help of a Thai grocer across the street and a few English words from the restaurant's altogether admirable cook, we imitated the previous evening's delicacies at home.

What was the food like? Well, let me give Thai cookery my highest praise, reserved only for four-star cuisines and better: it tastes like *food*. Or to put it even more extravagantly, it tastes exactly like what God must have had in mind when he invented the subject in the first place. It really is that good. Many of its concoctions are fiery; but if you make them yourself, it's your hand that holds the chili peppers, so there never has to be more heat than you can stand.

I urge Thai cooking upon you, then. Begin with the quintessentially typical Thai Steak Salad — the Yam of Beef (pronounced "yum") — from the recipes that follow: it will make an instant convert of you. Hurry, though. If homemade Thai food isn't the next culinary enthusiasm of the fadding crowd, I'll eat my old-timer's hat: there are only about two weeks left before every kid on the block will be able to say *yum*.

Note. In these recipes, Thai ingredients available in oriental groceries are marked with an asterisk.* (Spellings, by the way, tend to vary wildly on the labels. If something looks even close, it's probably the right item. Also, the names given the dishes differ from restaurant to restaurant: the noodle dish Mee, for example, is sometimes Mee Siam, Mee Krob or Pad Thai.)

RUM
(Minced Pork in Egg Crêpes)

FOR THE CRÊPES

4 large eggs
4 teaspoons water
Salt to taste
Lard or peanut oil for frying

Beat the first three ingredients together lightly in a bowl. Heat an omelet pan or small skillet thoroughly and add about 1 tablespoon lard. Holding the bowl over the pan, dip your hand in the egg mixture, and then let the egg mixture run off your fingers into the pan. Move your hand as you do this so a lacy pattern is formed. Repeat until the bottom of the pan is well covered with a "net." Remove the crêpe to a plate, and make additional crêpes until the egg is used up.

FOR THE FILLING

½ pound ground pork
1 head pickled garlic,* peeled and minced

Fish sauce* (*nam pla*) to taste
Sugar to taste
Chopped coriander to taste
Red chili peppers, seeded and chopped, to taste

Fry the pork in a little fat until lightly browned, and season it with the remaining ingredients.

To make the dish, spread one of the egg "nets" on a board, put about 2 tablespoons of the pork mixture in the center and fold the net over it, making a neat package. Repeat with remaining pork and egg. *Makes about 8 packages.*

About coconut cream and milk. These unsweetened liquids are central to Thai cooking. While the canned product is usable (but expensive), it is never as good as what you can make yourself. Note, however, that the emulsified, sweetened "coconut cream" sold for piña coladas and other purposes *cannot* be used in these recipes.

In order of declining excellence, here are four ways of providing yourself with the real things.

1. Break open a large coconut. To do this, set it on its side and, using the back of a cleaver or heavy knife, hit it sharply on the "parallel of latitude" that your eye draws about one third of the way down from the end with the three "eyes." Rotate the coconut as you continue striking so that the cleaver hits all the way around the parallel of latitude. The coconut will break quite nicely into two unequal "cups." Discard — or drink — the liquid inside.

Pry the meat away from the shell (peeling away the brown skin, but only if you're a purist), break it into chunks that your food processor (or blender) will accept, and process it with the sharp blade until it is finely grated. (Alternatively, grate it on a grater.) Next, add 2 cups warm water to the processor and let it run for several minutes. Line a sieve with a double layer of cheesecloth, empty the processor into it, and squeeze out all the liquid you can. This is coconut cream. To make coconut milk, reprocess the coconut pulp with another 1 or 2 cups warm water and squeeze it out as before.

2. Buy frozen coconut meat from an oriental grocer and process as above.

3. Buy frozen coconut milk from the same grocer, thaw, and use.

4. Use desiccated coconut and process as above, using a bit more water the first time around.

COCONUT CHICKEN SOUP WITH GALANGA

Galanga, a rhizome of the ginger family, has a taste like nothing else. It is sold already sliced and dried, and keeps indefinitely in a covered jar.

2½ cups coconut cream made from 1 large coconut
    (see above)
7 or 8 pieces *galanga**
½ teaspoon peppercorns
½ teaspoon coriander stems (or roots) pounded together
    in a mortar with the peppercorns
Salt to taste
2 or 3 skinned fillets of raw chicken breast sliced into
    bite-size pieces

ACCOMPANIMENT

1 tablespoon *namprik pao**
Fish sauce* (*nam pla*) to taste
Lime juice to taste (start with 2 teaspoons)
Sugar to taste (start with 2 teaspoons)

Boil the first five ingredients together until slightly reduced. Just before serving, add the sliced chicken and cook only 1 or 2 minutes — that is, until barely done. Mix ingredients of the accompaniment and pass with the soup — and put out additional fish sauce, lime juice and sugar for those who would like to add more. *Serves 4 as a first course.*

MEE
(Rice Vermicelli with Shrimp)

This is basically a leftover dish: shredded cooked pork, chicken and crabmeat (about ¼ cup each) can be added if you have them.

½ pound Thai rice stick noodles* (fine, not broad)
½ cup peanut oil
1 teaspoon minced garlic
½ pound peeled, deveined fresh shrimp
1 tablespoon dried shrimp,* soaked 15 minutes in warm water
1 tablespoon sugar, or more, to taste
1 tablespoon fish sauce* (*nam pla*) or more, to taste
1 tablespoon ketchup, or more, to taste
2 eggs
1 cup bean sprouts

AS GARNISHES

Raw bean sprouts
Chopped scallions
Sliced red onion
Coriander leaves
Crushed red chili peppers
Lemon wedges
Crushed peanuts

Soak the noodles in hot water for 1 minute and drain.

Heat the peanut oil in a skillet or wok, add the garlic, let it color slightly, and then add the fresh and dried shrimp. Cook until the fresh shrimp are barely done.

Add the sugar, fish sauce and ketchup, and stir everything together. Break the eggs into the pan, and stir gently, breaking up the yolks, until the egg begins to set. Add the noodles, and toss until they are uniformly orange. Add the bean sprouts (and other meats, if any), and cook 2 minutes more.

Serve on a platter with the garnishes attractively arranged. *Serves 4.*

THAI GREEN CURRY WITH PORK

2 tablespoons lard or peanut oil
1 or 2 envelopes Thai green curry paste° — or 1 or 2
    tablespoons, if you buy the paste in a jar or can
    (*Note.* Most Thai curries are distinguished by naming
    them after colors. The finished dishes, however, some-
    times bear little resemblance to the color in the name.
    Also, Indian curry powder is *not* a substitute for Thai
    pastes.)
½ pound lean raw pork sliced into thin, bite-size pieces
2 cups coconut cream (see above)
2 tablespoons fish sauce° (*nam pla*)
Lime juice to taste
Sugar to taste
2 green chili peppers, seeded and cut lengthwise into strips
1 cup shelled peas (or whole, edible-pod peas, if available)
Crushed peanuts

Heat the fat in a deep skillet or wok and stir-fry the curry paste
for 1 or 2 minutes. Add the pork and fish sauce, and stir-fry until
the pork is cooked through. Add the coconut cream, sugar and
lime juice, and boil until the liquid is slightly reduced. Add the
chili peppers and peas, and cook briefly. Garnish with crushed
peanuts.

Serve with plain white rice. *Serves 2 to 4.*

YAM OF BEEF
(Thai Steak Salad)

FOR THE SALAD

1 medium head romaine or other leaf lettuce, broken up
1 red onion, sliced thin into lengthwise strips
4 scallions (green parts, too) cut into ¼-inch pieces
1 cucumber, peeled, halved lengthwise, seeded, and
    sliced crosswise
Fresh basil leaves to taste
Fresh mint leaves to taste

Fresh coriander leaves to taste
Fresh red chili peppers, seeded and sliced (or crushed
    dried peppers), to taste

FOR THE DRESSING

⅔ cup fish sauce
⅓ cup lime juice
1 teaspoon (or more) minced garlic
2 teaspoons dried lemon grass* (if fresh is available,
    by all means use it — sliced fine slantwise)
Dried red chili peppers, crushed, to taste (if not
    included above)

FOR THE STEAK

1 beefsteak (of a size suitable for two persons —
    tenderized, if necessary)

Combine the salad ingredients in a large bowl and mix well.
Combine the dressing ingredients in a jar and shake well.
Grill the steak rare.
Pour half the dressing over the salad ingredients and toss
well. Turn out onto a platter.
Slice the steak into thin, bite-size pieces, toss them in the
remaining dressing, arrange them on top of the salad, and pour
the rest of the dressing over all. *Serves 4.*

SANKHAYA
(Thai Coconut Cream Dessert)

2 cups thick coconut cream (made with warm water scented
    with rose petals, if you like; remove petals before
    processing)
½ cup light brown sugar
1 cup white sugar
¼ cup cooked frozen or canned corn (or the same amount
    of diced cooked taro or sweet potato)
1 envelope unsweetened gelatine
2 tablespoons sugar

Boil the first four ingredients together until sugar is well dissolved and liquid is slightly reduced. Add the gelatine, mixed with 2 tablespoons sugar, and dissolve thoroughly. Cool slightly and pour into suitable parfait glasses, distributing the vegetable evenly among them. Allow to stand undisturbed until cool (the coconut fat will rise to the top); then refrigerate until set. *Serves 4 to 6.*

This recipe, incidentally, makes a fine custard. Simply omit the vegetable and replace the gelatine with 6 eggs, beaten well. (Allow the coconut cream–sugar mixture to cool considerably before adding the eggs.) Pour the finished mixture into a small, hollowed-out pumpkin (or small, hollowed-out acorn squashes, or a pie plate, or custard cups) and bake at 325° to 350° until set (35 minutes to 1 hour or more, depending on the container chosen).

23

An Italian Sauce-out

Of all the foreign foods that have entered so freely into American cookery, none has made itself more at home than pasta. There's hardly a market anywhere without at least a dozen different shapes on the shelves, and it's a rare household that doesn't see at least one of them on the table several times a month. Add to that the fact that pasta is not just a carbohydrate stand-in for potatoes but a cereal food with the goodness of grain, and you have one of the happiest immigration stories on record.

On the sad side, though, our Americanization of it has neglected two of pasta's most winsome qualities: its ability to appear in literally hundreds of guises, and its adaptability to short-order cooking. On the one hand, we overserve a single shape, spaghetti, so much so that in common speech the name does duty for all the rest. Not only that, but we sauce it with a single color, red; we flavor it with a single herb, oregano; and we limit our gustatory enjoyment of it to a single kind of service, the at-home supper, where, with nothing more than a salad, it makes up the whole meal. On the other hand, and paradoxically, we renege on that simplicity when it comes to the kinds of sauce we make: almost everybody's favorite recipe calls for long simmering. What might have been a quick and easy meal is turned into an afternoon's pot-watching.

The recipes given here make a break with all five of those unnecessary — and, if you're really talking Italian — inauthentic limitations. To begin with, they suggest using a variety of shapes. With no food more than pasta does diversity of texture make such a difference on the palate. Thin sauces, because they need a great deal of surface to adhere to, cry out for the finest of long strands: vermicelli or cappellini (sometimes called, with typical Italian extravagance, *capelli d'angeli* — "angel hair"). By contrast, thick sauces, with their greater natural adhesiveness, go better with chunky shapes.

Next, the sauces that follow come in a variety of colors: green, white and red for the Italian flag, and red/green, pale yellow and honey beige for equally Italian good measure. More than that, they have a diversity of flavors: basil, parsley, zucchini, lemon, nutmeg, roasted peppers, egg, bacon and anchovy all have a place in the list. Still more, each one makes a fine first course for a company meal, especially if the main course — say, a roast chicken — won't be enough for the crowd you have to feed.

But finally and best of all, every one of them can be made quickly — so quickly, in fact, that the time between putting the water on to boil and getting the cooked pasta out of the pot is quite sufficient for the average cook to make even two of them at once.

Here they are. *Buon appetito!*

PESTO

6 to 8 shelled brazil nuts (or an equivalent amount of pine
    nuts, if you're rich)
6 tablespoons good Italian-style grating cheese
2 cloves peeled garlic (or to taste)
Olive oil (about 1 cup, more or less)

2 cups fresh basil leaves, or 1 cup basil leaves and 1 cup
    fresh parsley (this sauce cannot be made with dried
    herbs; frozen basil leaves, however, make excellent
    pesto — *see page 50*)
Salt to taste
1 or 2 tablespoons boiling water from the pasta pot

Put the first three ingredients into an electric blender (a food processor can be used, but it will not make as smooth a sauce) and run it briefly to grate them.

Add about ½ cup oil, and run the blender to purée the mixture.

With the blender still running, put in all the leaves and force them down into the blades carefully with a wooden spoon (a rubber spatula may sound like a better idea, but bits of it all too easily incorporate themselves into the pesto).

Add more oil gradually, the blender still running, until the mixture is like a thick mayonnaise. Add salt to taste, turn off the blender, and let it stand.

Just before you drain the pasta, start the blender again, add 1 or 2 tablespoons boiling pasta water, blend until smooth, and empty into a serving dish. *Serves 4 to 6* — over margherite, perhaps.

ZUCCHINI SAUCE

¼ cup butter
4 to 6 small zucchini, sliced thin
Lemon juice to taste (try ½ lemon to start)
Freshly grated nutmeg to taste (try ¼ teaspoon to start)
¼ cup chopped parsley
Salt to taste
½ pint heavy cream

Melt the butter in a saucepan, add the zucchini, and cook over high heat, stirring often, for a few minutes.

Add the next four ingredients and cook, still over high heat and stirring, until the zucchini slices are barely tender.

Add the cream, boil hard to reduce it a bit, check the salt, and spoon over hot, drained rotelle. *Serves 4 to 6.*

UNCOOKED TOMATO SAUCE
(See page 15)

ROASTED GREEN PEPPER SAUCE

4 large green bell peppers
3 tablespoons butter
3 tablespoons olive oil
1 medium onion, sliced
Salt and pepper to taste
6 fresh tomatoes (or the equivalent, canned), peeled
    and chopped

Holding the peppers one by one on a long roasting fork, singe them over a gas flame until they are black all over. Flick off the burnt skin (the small amount that inevitably remains is part of the flavor of the dish). Slice the peppers thin.

Melt the olive oil and butter together in a saucepan, add the onion, and cook until soft and golden.

Add the peppers, simmer till they give up most of their moisture, and add salt and pepper to taste.

Add the tomatoes, and simmer until everything is tender and the sauce is reduced to a good consistency. Correct the seasoning and serve with hot, drained perciatelli. *Serves 4 to 6.*

CARBONARA SAUCE

This dish can be prepared completely in the kitchen and presented in a single serving bowl. The version given here, however, allows guests to do their own mixing at the table. The only thing the cook needs to do at the last minute is move fast.

It's the heat of the pasta — and the bowl — that "cooks" the egg: both therefore need to be brought to the table promptly.

PER GUEST (AT EACH PLACE)

3 strips fried bacon
1 beaten egg in a small cup

FOR ALL (ON THE TABLE)

Hot individual soup bowls
Bowl of chopped parsley
Bowl of grated cheese
Salt and pepper
1 pound hot cappellini, cooked, and tossed with a little
    hot olive oil

Bring the hot cappellini and hot individual soup bowls to the table. Divide the pasta into the bowls, and serve. Then sit, pour your egg over your own serving, break up the bacon onto it, help yourself to parsley and cheese, mix it all together, and invite your guests to follow your example. *Serves 4 to 6.*

ANCHOVY BUTTER

The all-time simplest sauce in the world.

¼ pound butter at room temperature
Anchovy paste to taste

Put the butter in a small mixing bowl and squeeze some anchovy paste out of the tube onto it. Beat them together until well blended, mix into hot, drained linguine, and garnish with chopped parsley. *Serves 4 to 6.*

As I think about it, though, I simply have to add two more recipes. The first is for yet another short-order sauce, but the second is for a side dish. It is, hands down, the best version of stuffed artichokes I know — cadged, appropriately enough, from a lady who is a superb Italian cook.

VEAL OR PORK PIZZAIOLA

½ cup olive oil
3 cloves garlic, peeled
½ can flat anchovy fillets
½ teaspoon red pepper
1 cup Italian parsley
½ pound veal or pork, cut into thin julienne strips
6 black and 6 green olives, pitted and quartered
2 tablespoons white wine
1 cup tomato sauce
1 cup brown stock
Oregano to taste
Pepper to taste
Salt, if necessary
1 pound fusilli, cooked and drained

Put the first five ingredients in a blender and purée thoroughly.

Put 4 tablespoons of the purée (reserving the rest for another use) into a large skillet, place over high heat and, when it is hot, sauté the meat strips for 3 or 4 minutes.

Add the next seven ingredients, bring to a boil, and simmer several minutes.

Toss the fusilli with the sauce. *Serves 4 to 6.*

STUFFED ARTICHOKES

6 fresh artichokes
2 cups bread crumbs
1 cup finely shredded Italian-style cheese
½ cup chopped fresh parsley
3 cloves garlic, minced
1 tablespoon oregano
½ teaspoon pepper
6 cloves garlic, cut in half
Water
Salt to taste
¼ cup olive oil (or to taste)

With one push of a sharp, heavy knife, cut off the upper part of each artichoke at a point 1 to 1½ inches from the top. With a pair of scissors, snip off the tops of the remaining outside leaves below that point. Cut the stem off, making a flat base. Using a sharp spoon, dig out the center leaves and the "choke."

Mix the next six ingredients in a large bowl.

Take each trimmed artichoke and, standing it in the bowl of seasoned crumbs, spread the leaves apart with your fingers and force in as much of the crumb mixture as it will hold.

Stand the artichokes in a large pot, sprinkle the garlic pieces around the bottom, add water to a depth of 1 inch, salt to taste, drizzle the olive oil over the tops, and simmer, covered, for 30 minutes or until tender. Serve hot or lukewarm, passing some of the cooking liquid at the table. *Serves 6.*

24

A Thanksgiving Refresher

"Yes, but . . ." the Palate objected.

"Kindly do not interrupt when your betters are speaking," the Mind replied. "Thanksgiving is the perfect holiday. Consider first its brilliant choice of the optimum time of the week. Any day other than Thursday would be a disaster: Tuesday, for example, would drag three dreary workdays in its train; Sunday, five. And Saturday? Saturday has the only free time not followed by a resumption of the grind. Why clog it with maiden aunts, Dutch uncles and screaming children?"

"Yes, but . . ."

"But me no buts. Thanksgiving is also superior to all other federally finagled four-day weekends. G. A. Lincolnton's Non-birthday, for example, and the unmemorable Memorial Day weekend are mere vacancies in time. Whatever corporate observances they once involved have been subsumed into a distracted indulgence in purely personal enthusiasms. A nation of people doing their own things can hardly pretend to have a national observance of any one thing. Thanksgiving, by contrast, has not only a common theme but a common ritual as well."

"Yes. However . . ."

"However me no howevers either. July Fourth and Labor

Day are worse yet. They are nothing but boundary markers delimiting the desert that is summer — arbitrary brackets, as it were, enclosing a parenthetical season with no redeeming liturgical significance."

"Yes. Still . . ."

"Advert me no adversatives at all. Thanksgiving is better even than Chanukah, Christmas, Passover or Easter. Those festivities, while they involve unifying activities, are enjoyable chiefly in anticipation; the feasts themselves are letdowns. Advent, for instance, is fun: it has, in Christmas, a future that informs and brightens each dark December day. But when December twenty-fifth finally rolls around, it is simply a present with no future whatsoever to look forward to. Thanksgiving, however, has Advent, Chanukah and Christmas waiting to burst in the minute the dishwasher is loaded. Therefore Thanksgiving is the best of all possible holidays."

"Yes. Nevertheless . . ."

"Dear me! I suppose there is nothing for it but to let you speak. What is this cavil that is festering in your mind?"

"If the holiday is really all that great, how come everybody eats turkey?"

"What's wrong with turkey?"

"The question is, What's right with it? The only thing worse is crow."

"I find turkey perfectly acceptable. Why, Benjamin Franklin actually wanted to make it the national bird. Do you question the judgment of the mind that discovered electricity?"

"Turkey may be a bright idea to a Mind, but to a Palate, it's a dim bulb. Even roast eagle would probably taste better . . ."

But enough: both faculties have their points. Thanksgiving is indeed the nearest thing we have to a national liturgy. From sea to shining sea, it calls forth a grand harmony of groaning boards: mashed potatoes overflow everywhere with gravy, turnips abound, buttered parsnips do more for mouths than fine words — and kale, swiss chard, red cabbage and onions, plus two stuffings, three kinds of cranberry sauce and a minimum of four pies all join their contrapuntal voices to the song.

And yet. What must we think of a nation that, as the central motif of this gustatory concerto, insists upon a bird that has a name used chiefly as an insult — and that, when it is finally released from its dimwitted existence, is uncookable, uncarvable and inedible? Is not some nationwide liturgical renewal in order? Should we not at least do penance for this gastronomic cardinal sin?

"Ah, but," you say. "Turkey can be roasted so that all its parts are properly done; it can be carved without undue incident; and it is, after all, eaten — often in vast quantities. Is that not proof enough of its acceptability?"

No. Reconsider your points in order.

Turkey can be cooked properly. Of course it can; but by the same token, so can Kleenex be embroidered. The question to be asked in both cases is: Is the original material worth the effort? Do the benefits warrant the cost? Specifically, does the taste of a turkey in any way repay the jockeying, pulling and hauling required to roast it in four different positions of recumbency — on both sides, upside down, and right side up? It does not.

Turkey can be carved without incident. If you are referring to a turkey roasted for the express purpose of being photographed while being carved, you are of course right. But then, photographers are careful to show you only one or two moist slices of breast meat falling neatly from the knife. In real life, such a bird would most likely have leg meat the consistency of a rubber duck. And if perchance the thighs were done to tender, well-cooked perfection, even the best carver in the world would be hard put to keep the breast from looking as if it had been kicked apart with a combat boot.

Turkeys are in fact eaten enthusiastically. So too are diner pies, factory doughnuts and canned spaghetti. End of rebuttal. On to renewal.

If not turkey, then what?

It would probably be unseemly for the author of this book to manifest more than passing enthusiasm for a capon, so let that delightful possibility be mentioned only for the record. There is of course duck — or better said, ducks: one duck, though delicious, doth not a Thanksgiving dinner make. There is also goose; but even Bob Cratchit's glorious bird goes hardly once around a long table. And, admittedly, there are game birds — but now we have abandoned all semblance of a unifying, nationwide liturgy and entered the solemn high but sectarian rites of the gun club.

What, then? Why, roast chicken. In this country we are currently blessed not only with mountain majesties and fruited plains but with excellent seven- or eight-pound roasters as well — with generous birds that at least have an American's chance of turning out evenly cooked. Two of them will serve all but a horde; and they will not only fit into the oven but also provide a moist and proper home for the obligatory two stuffings. Gone will be the days of the second stuffing in the bread pan, either dried out or swimming in fat. Gone the Hobson's choice between desiccated breast and blood-rare thigh. Gone the soul-destroying insincerity by which each year's unvarying disappointment is proclaimed "the best turkey ever." Gone, in short, everything that should never have come in the first place.

Accordingly, since it is far harder to roast a chicken badly than to do a turkey well, here is one of the few lists of Thanksgiving recipes whose centerpiece is not a lesson on how to teach acrobatics to a bird. It consists simply of some fresh suggestions on the too often neglected subject of the "trimmings" that actually make up most of the meal. There are seven ideas for stuffings, nine for vegetables and, as if anyone needed them, even a couple of advices on desserts.

There is not a word here, though, about apple pie. That subject is a trap into which no wary food writer should fall: for even if, as a people, we have erred in our choice of the main course for Thanksgiving dinner, we have always ended the meal with the pie than which nothing is more American — and for which every red-blooded citizen has the best recipe ever. Only a fool would try to teach such a nation of grandmothers to suck eggs.

In any case, though, Happy Thanksgiving to all — and to turkey, goodnight.

OYSTER STUFFING

6 tablespoons chicken fat (or more, to taste)
½ cup celery, chopped
4 scallions, chopped
Crushed savory to taste
1 pint shucked oysters, with liquid
Salt, white pepper and red pepper to taste
3 to 4 cups cubed day-old white bread
½ cup chopped parsley

Heat the chicken fat in a deep skillet, add the next three ingredients, and sauté for a few minutes. Add the oysters with their liquid, and sauté briefly until their edges curl. Add salt, white pepper and red pepper to taste, turn off the heat, add the bread cubes and parsley, and toss the mixture thoroughly. Check the seasoning, and stuff and truss the chicken.

VARIATIONS

1. *Shrimp or scallop.* Use thyme in place of savory, and sauté cut-up raw shrimp, or fresh bay scallops, or cut-up sea scallops

in place of the oysters. Add more melted chicken fat or a little chicken stock if you like a moister stuffing.

2. *Mushroom.* Use thyme as well as savory, and sauté 2 cups cut-up fresh mushrooms in place of the seafood. Add Madeira (or sherry) before tossing with the bread and parsley.

SAUSAGE STUFFING

2 cups bulk breakfast sausage meat
2 medium onions, chopped
1 or 2 ribs celery, chopped
Poultry seasoning to taste
Salt and pepper to taste
3 to 4 cups cubed day-old white bread
½ cup chopped parsley
Melted chicken fat, or chicken stock

Brown the sausage meat in a deep skillet, breaking it up but still leaving coarse chunks.

Add the onion and celery and sauté briefly.

Add the poultry seasoning, salt and pepper, turn off the heat, add the bread and parsley, and toss the mixture thoroughly. Moisten with fat or stock, if desired. Check the seasoning, and stuff and truss the chicken.

VARIATIONS

1. *With Italian sausage.* As the sausage browns, deglaze the pan several times with splashes of dry vermouth, or dry white or red white. Use basil in place of poultry seasoning — or use a mixture of basil, marjoram, rosemary and thyme. Use sesame-covered bread — or break up a few sesame bread sticks and add them to the stuffing.

2. *With nuts.* To either of the above, add broken-up nutmeats as desired: roasted, peeled chestnuts, or pecans, or pignoli, or brazil nuts.

3. *With giblets.* Boil hearts and gizzards till tender; chop them and add to any of the above. Sauté livers briefly in the sausage fat, cut them into pieces, and add likewise.

FRIED POTATOES, GREEK STYLE

6 medium-size baking potatoes, washed but not peeled, and
    cut up as for large French fries
Juice of ½ lemon (or more, to taste)
Salt and pepper to taste
Oregano to taste
½ cup olive oil

In a bowl, combine the potatoes with the lemon juice and spices, mix well, and allow them to marinate for an hour or so.

Heat the olive oil in a wok or deep skillet over high heat until it begins to smoke. Add the marinated potatoes, and fry them, tossing gently but often, until they begin to brown. Check the seasoning, adding additional salt, pepper, lemon juice and oregano, as desired.

Cook until nicely browned and just tender. Do not let them get so soft that they fall apart.

BRUSSELS SPROUTS WITH GARLIC AND CHEESE

4 cups fresh Brussels sprouts
¼ to ½ cup butter, as desired
2 or 3 cloves garlic, crushed (or to taste)
Lemon juice to taste
Grated Italian-style cheese to taste

Cook the Brussels sprouts, uncovered, in water salted to taste until they are just tender, not soft. Drain, shock under cold water, drain again, and set aside till needed.

Melt the butter in a deep pot over low heat, sauté the garlic briefly until soft but not browned, stir in some lemon juice, and set aside till needed.

At the last minute, heat the butter-garlic-lemon mixture, add the Brussels sprouts, and toss gently till heated through. Add the grated cheese, toss lightly once again, and serve.

VARIATION

Brussels sprouts with sesame-mustard dressing. In a small, dry pot, toast ¼ cup unhulled white sesame seeds (available in oriental groceries) over moderate heat. Shake them constantly until you hear seven of them "pop." Empty them into a *suribachi* (Japanese mortar), or into a spice grinder, and grind them to powder. Put the ground sesame into a bowl and mix it to a thin paste with the following: 2 tablespoons rice vinegar, 2 tablespoons soy sauce, 1 tablespoon sugar, 1 teaspoon saké, salt to taste, and 1 teaspoon hot mustard prepared from powder mixed with water to the consistency of heavy cream. Toss with Brussels sprouts that have been warmed in butter or oil, and serve.

BROCCOLI WITH LEMON SOY

2 bunches broccoli
Butter, olive oil, or peanut oil to taste
Lemon juice and soy sauce, mixed in equal parts, to taste

Remove the florets from the broccoli and cut the stems into thin slices crosswise — or reserve the stems for another use.

Stir-fry the broccoli pieces in butter or oil in a wok or deep skillet over high heat, adding judicious splashes of the lemon-soy mixture, to taste, as you proceed. Cook only until they are just tender. Check the seasoning and serve.

VARIATION

Broccoli with ginger soy. Grate about an inch of fresh ginger root on the finest hand grater available. Put the pulp into a tea strainer, and press out the juice into a cup. Add soy sauce to taste, and use as above, in place of lemon soy.

SWISS CHARD WITH SCALLIONS

1 large bunch Swiss chard, with stems, washed
Butter or olive oil to taste
1 bunch scallions, cut into ¼-inch lengths
Salt and pepper to taste

Cut the Swiss chard into large pieces, plunge it into boiling
water, and cook it until the stems are just tender. Drain, shock
under cold water, and drain again. Squeeze out as much water
as possible, put the chard on a board, and chop it up with a
large knife.

Melt the butter or olive oil in a deep pot, add the scallions,
and cook them over moderate heat until just tender.

Add the chopped chard, toss well, season to taste, and
serve.

CAULIFLOWER WITH CINNAMON

Juice of one lemon
1 large head cauliflower
½ cup butter
1 teaspoon ground cinnamon (or to taste)
½ teaspoon ground nutmeg (or to taste)
Salt and white pepper to taste
1 cup soft bread crumbs
1 pint heavy cream

Put cold water into a large bowl and mix in the lemon juice.

Remove the center stalk from the cauliflower, cut the head
into large, thin slices, and put them in the lemon water.

Butter a suitable au gratin dish liberally. Drain the cauliflower slices, place half of them in the bottom of the dish, and
sprinkle them with half the cinnamon, nutmeg, salt, pepper,
and bread crumbs. Dot with half the remaining butter and pour
half the cream on top. Make a second layer, using all remaining
ingredients. Cover, and bake at 375° for 1 hour or until done.

PIE IDEAS

Topping. In place of the usual whipped cream or ice cream on pumpkin, mince or apple pie, use cold sour cream that has been seasoned to taste with fine granulated sugar and vanilla (or vanilla and dark rum).

Mince pie filling. Fry up some very finely diced (not ground) raw beef — or venison, if you can lay your hands on any — in kidney suet or butter, adding salt and allspice while it cooks; then flame it with cognac, add homemade green-tomato mince-meat, or commercial mincemeat, and simmer, covered, for an hour or so.

Lemon meringue pie. Since most people taste only dreadful commercial productions, why not add a good homemade version to your list? Just be sure a) to put the cold filling into the pre-baked pie shell at the last minute, b) to swirl on the meringue in dramatic peaks, and c) to brown it quickly in a very hot oven.

Pumpkin pie. Don't be afraid to play wildly with ingredients. A filling that is spiced predominantly with ginger or orange, for example, makes a welcome change. So does one made not from pumpkin at all, but from baked butternut squash.

Epilogue

Well, everything, in a way. Of the making of cookbooks especially there is no end. The preparation and presentation of food is endlessly fascinating — and it is perhaps the best, cheapest hobby in the world. There are no club dues or chic clothes; it does not require undue time or special reservations; it uses only equipment you have to have anyway; and it does not clutter up closets with the memorabilia of abandoned enthusiasms. The products of its successes happily disappear, and the evidence of its failures can always be destroyed by feeding them to the cats. It is a pursuit so perpetually renewable that even a long life is not time enough for all that can be said about it.

But on the other hand, there is probably next to nothing that needs adding here. If your reading of this book has been anything like the root-and-branch refreshment of cookery that its researching and writing have been, we can all be left to fend famously for ourselves. I urge therefore only two things upon you.

The first is that you never stop cultivating the virtue of paying attention to the uniqueness of every last edible morsel that comes before you. The world we live in exists not because it is an old inventory item once made and long since shelved, but because each several scrap of its marvelous being is an intimate and immediate response to the Creator who, at every moment, romances it out of nothing into existence by loving regard. Saint Thomas Aquinas once said that if God wanted to destroy the world, he wouldn't have to do anything; he would have to *stop* doing something. So too with cookery. The only sin that can ever turn it sour is boredom: stay fascinated, and you will cook well forever.

The other bit of advice flows straight from that: don't be afraid to *play* — even to fiddle around — when you cook. God, as I said at the beginning of this book, does exactly that when he creates. Take the case of the *Solanaceae*, or nightshade family. Who but a Mind utterly committed to fiddling with new variations on old themes would have come up with comestible nightshades like peppers, tomatoes, eggplants and potatoes; with inedible, but still delightful creatures such as tobacco, petunias and salpiglossis; and, for paradoxical, wickedly amusing good measure, with the deadly nightshade itself, the poisonous but healing *Atropa belladonna*? I simply want to encourage you — within less ambitious limits, of course — to follow the example of that Divine Fooling Around.

Indeed, I can think of no more fitting close for this book than to give you two of my own best bits of culinary fiddling during the summer of its composition: Eggplant with Uncooked Tomato Sauce, and Cold Lo Mein with Crisp-fried Garden Vegetables. Since we are friends now in the saving foolishness, permit me to describe them to you as just one cook to another.

I. Take some small eggplants (I plant the miniature Japanese varieties, but any will do), cut them up to resemble fat French fries, and soak them in salted cold water for 15 minutes.

Meanwhile, make up some Uncooked Tomato Sauce, as on page 15.

Drain the eggplant pieces, pat them with a towel, and put them all into a large paper bag containing some salted and peppered flour. Shake them well to coat them with flour, empty them out onto a cake cooling rack, and jostle them about to get rid of excess flour.

Fry batches of the eggplant pieces in a wok containing a cup or so of very hot olive oil, tossing them gently until they are all nicely browned. To each batch add some thinly sliced onion during the last few minutes of frying.

Layer half of the hot eggplant and onion mixture in the bottom of a suitable dish, spread on half of the tomato sauce, add the rest of the eggplant, and top it with the rest of the tomato sauce. Press it down lightly, and serve hot, lukewarm or cold, as you like.

II. Cook ½ pound Chinese noodles (or linguine) al dente, drain, rinse in cold water till cool, drain again, and reserve.

Stir-fry ½ pound bean sprouts quickly in sesame oil, seasoning them with soy sauce, saké, brown bean sauce and cut chives. Cool.

Mix the bean sprouts into the noodles, add lots of coriander leaves and additional sesame oil, soy sauce, and so forth, plus salt and pepper, all to taste. Refrigerate.

Cut up an assortment of garden vegetables into julienne strips: ½ cup each, for example, of eggplant, zucchini, scallions and sweet red or green peppers, all cut into ³⁄₁₆-by-³⁄₁₆-by-1½-inch pieces; ½ cup of broccoli florets, cut more or less to match; ¼ cup each of hot peppers and fresh ginger, cut into finer julienne strips.

Soak some shelled Brazil nuts in hot water for 5 minutes and slice them thin lengthwise.

Put the nuts and vegetables in a large bowl and season

them with sprinklings of soy sauce, saké, peanut oil, sugar, salt and pepper, all to taste. Mix and let stand for 15 minutes.

Heat 2 quarts of oil to deep-frying temperature.

Meanwhile, put a generous amount of cornstarch in the bottom of a large paper bag, mix the vegetables with the seasonings once again and, shaking the bag constantly, drop the vegetables into it by small handfuls so that they do not stick to each other. Empty the bag out onto a rack and move the vegetables about gently to get rid of excess cornstarch.

Put them into the hot oil all at once and fry, stirring often, for 4 or 5 minutes, or until crisp but not burnt. At the end, add ½ cup coriander leaves, fry for 20 to 30 seconds more, remove the vegetables from the oil, and drain on paper.

Arrange the noodle mixture on a large platter, top it with the fried vegetables, garnish the dish with lemon wedges, and serve.

There! Go and do thou likewise.

Index

Index